JOHN CALVIN

Selections from His Writings

Foreword by Marilynne Robinson

Translated by Elsie Anne McKee

Edited by Emilie Griffin

HarperSanFrancisco

A Division of HarperCollins*Publishers*

J. K. S. Reid's translation of "The Reply to Sadoleto" and "A Short Treatise on the Lord's Supper," from Calvin: Institutes of the Christian Religion (Library of Christian Classics Series) edited by John T. McNeill. Used by permission of Westminster John Knox Press.

Ford Lewis Battles's translation of the Institutes of the Christian Religion (Library of Christian Classics Series) edited by John T. McNeill. Used by permission of Westminster John Knox Press.

HarperCollins books may be purchased for educational, business, or sales promotional use. For information please write: Special Markets Department, HarperCollins Publishers, 10 East 53rd Street, New York, NY 10022.

HarperCollins Web site: http://www.harpercollins.com

HarperCollins®, ▰®, and HarperSanFrancisco™ are trademarks of HarperCollins Publishers

FIRST EDITION

Library of Congress Cataloging-in-Publication Data
Calvin, Jean, 1509–1564.
    [Selections. English. 2006]
    John Calvin : selections from his writings / foreword by Marilynne Robinson ;
translated by Elsie Anne McKee ; edited by Emilie Griffin. — 1st ed.
        p. cm.
    ISBN-13: 978–0–06–075467–9
    ISBN-10: 0–06–075467–2
        1. Christian life—Reformed authors. 2. Reformed Church—Doctrines. I. Title:
Selections from his writings. II. McKee, Elsie Anne. III. Griffin, Emilie. IV. Title.
BX9420.A32M23   2006
230'.42—dc22   2005052636

06 07 08 09 10 RRD(H) 10 9 8 7 6 5 4 3 2 1

CONTENTS

Foreword

Jean Calvin, the French Renaissance humanist and Reformation theologian known to the English-speaking world as John Calvin, has been extraordinarily influential and highly controversial since he published the *Institutes of the Christian Religion* in 1536 at the age of twenty-seven. However, outside the few special circles in which he is not only revered but also read, Calvin is often regarded as a religious authoritarian who imposed on his followers a regime of intolerance, prudery, obscurantism, and asceticism together with a passion for work based solidly on metaphysical angst. Those who comment on American history and culture tend to assign any unlikable aspect of it to the influence of Calvinism, which has caused Calvinism to be seen as a repository of regrettable biases and delusions, not only in the public mind, but also in the minds of the various learned who debate such topics. If we could disabuse ourselves of this notion of Calvinism as the explanation for whatever ails modern American culture, we could liberate the theologian and his thought from the encumbrances that make them unknown and unknowable to modern inquirers. Calvin as a disembodied glower would cease to be a factor in our thinking. Then he might emerge as what he was, a human being of exceptional gifts who, against his own wishes but as a consequence of his abilities, occupied a position of great influence during the European Reformation and long afterward.

From his childhood Jean Calvin was carefully and seriously educated, first for the priesthood, then for the law, then in classical

Latin literature as well as Hebrew and Greek. He was an early master of the French language and a major influence in its develop-
ment. He emerged as a voice of the Reformation with the publica-
tion of the Institutes, which he describes, in a preface addressed to
the king of France, as a defense of religious dissenters then being
burned in Paris. The "defense," he says, is an explication of their
views that will demonstrate the orthodoxy of their faith and the
heterodoxy of those who persecute them. Since the king himself
had authorized the persecutions, the implication was that he was
numbered among the heterodox.

Although Calvin was acquainted with and enjoyed influence
among members of the French royal family, he was nevertheless consistently dismissive of aristocracy. The city of Geneva, in
which he never held public office and of which he only became a
citizen five years before his death, had undergone a revolution before Calvin, anonymous and fugitive, passed through on his way
from northern Italy to the Reformed city of Strasbourg. Geneva
had thrown off its bishop and ruling family, the house of Savoy,
and was being governed by elected councils. Calvin was urged to
stay in Geneva to help consolidate the Reformation there. So his
deprecation of aristocracy as an institution would not have fallen
on ears unready to hear that message. And it is wholly consistent with the nonhierarchical church order he established, which
continues to be among the strongest aspects of his influence. His
was and is a church without princes. This is to be noted, because
historically he is often associated by his detractors with authori-
tarianism, with imposing his will on Geneva's civic and religious

life, when events indicate that he and the city were largely of one mind in these essential matters. Indeed, Calvin's design for the church was very likely influenced by the order already established in the government of the city when he arrived.

As for the city of Geneva, which Calvin is commonly said to have dominated or tyrannized, it is certainly true that his influence was very great and that his advice was called for continually, even in matters like the organization of the meat market. It is also true that he struggled continuously with the government of the city—and lost—in matters that seem securely within his purview, such as the frequency with which the churches should offer the sacrament of Communion. The city was small, ranging from ten thousand to fifteen or twenty thousand souls. The small size of the city would have been a factor in Calvin's prominence, since he preached and lectured several times every week and attended council meetings and meetings of clergy, he also established a faculty to teach the humanities and institutions for giving relief to the poor. He was, at the same time, one of the most prolific and widely read writers in Europe; he was in contact with significant figures all over the continent, trying to moderate passions and negotiate tolerance or protection for Protestant populations in France and elsewhere. This must certainly have enhanced his status in Geneva.

It is necessary to address Calvin himself, because the polemic against him has, over the centuries, become entrenched as history. As mentioned, the prevalent view of Calvin and Calvinism has very much influenced the interpretation of American history, stigmatizing seminal New England as gloomy and repressive, when, in its Calvinist period, it was strikingly liberal and reformist by comparison with the South and with Britain and Europe. The idea that it simply had to be gloomy is largely an extrapolation from the popular understanding of the doctrine of predestination. It should be noted, however, that Christian thinkers from Augustine to Calvin's contemporary Ignatius Loyola also believed in predestination, so this feature of his thought did not set him apart from the rest of Christendom, as people seem to assume.

The major challenge to this doctrine came from Jacobus Arminius, himself a Dutch Calvinist. It is clear from the writings of the eighteenth-century New England theologian Jonathan Edwards that the dispute with Arminianism was active in the American colonies. Edwards defends what he calls the Calvinist position—that is, predestination—but he treats the matter as a philosophical question, not as a question of dogma or orthodoxy. Indeed, it is characteristic of the Calvinist tradition that its disputes are internal, that it subdivides, and that it influences or blends with other traditions. The name "Calvinist" itself is shorthand for a complex and varied movement whose precursors Calvin first wrote to defend and whose thought has always been influenced by other theologians.

Yet Calvin looms as large he does because he ranks among the greatest theologians. He was a controversialist, as were other important figures of that contentious period, Martin Luther and Thomas More, for example. And this can be a distraction to modern readers, especially those not acquainted with the standards of that time. Calvin is so exceptional because, looking past the polemic, one finds a metaphysics of startling beauty. Calvin takes the individualism of Luther, the assertion that every believer is king, priest, and prophet, and develops it into an interpretation of reality centered in the individual perceiver. Mind, memory, senses—the human attributes that according to Calvin make us an image of God—are attuned to experiencing creation as in effect addressed to us, moment to moment, collectively and one by one. Perception is flawed by our Adamic sinfulness. But it is brilliant all the same and, by the grace of God, flooded with the beauty of the world God has made for us. There is nothing static in Calvin's universe, nothing fixed except by the will of God as consideration for our frailty.

—MARILYNNE ROBINSON

I. LIFE

1. The Reply to Sadoleto

In March 1539, Cardinal Jacopo Sadoleto, the highest-ranking
Roman Catholic priest in the neighborhood of Geneva, wrote
to the city, which had exiled William Farel and Calvin. His
pastoral letter, which was intended to draw them back from
heresy to allegiance to Rome, included a sketch of the kind of
justification he thought Calvin and his colleagues would make
before God's judgment seat for their acts in leaving Rome. The
leaders of Geneva concluded that they had no one capable of
answering Sadoleto's letter, so they sent it to Calvin in Strasbourg with a request that he reply. In the course of his answer,
Calvin defended his calling and faith by sketching why he had
felt compelled to do what he did, both as a minister and as a
Christian believer, responding to what he regarded as Sadoleto's
caricature with the same kind of first-person speech the cardinal had used. This is not strictly an autobiographical statement,
but it is very illuminating for the kinds of experiences and
convictions that led Calvin himself to break with Rome. The
translation is by J. K. S. Reid.

—E. A. McKee

But since toward the end a person has been introduced to plead
our cause, and you have cited us as defenders to the tribunal
of God, I have no hesitation in calling upon you to meet me
there. For such is our consciousness of the truth of our doctrine,
that it has no dread of the heavenly Judge, from whom we do
not doubt that it proceeded. But it dwells not on those frivolities

with which it has pleased you to amuse yourself, but which are certainly very much out of place. For what could be more inopportune than to come into the presence of God and to set about devising I know not what follies and framing for us an absurd defense which must immediately fail? In pious minds, whenever that day is suggested, the impression made is too solemn to leave them at leisure so to amuse themselves. Therefore, frivolity set aside, let us think of that day which human minds ought always to expect with suspense. And let us remember that, although desirable to the faithful, it may well be alarming to the ungodly and profane and those who despise God. Let us turn our ears to the sound of that trumpet which even the ashes of the dead will hear in their tombs. Let us direct our thoughts and minds to that Judge who, by the mere brightness of His countenance, will disclose whatever lurks in darkness, lay open all the secrets of the human heart, and crush all the wicked by the mere breath of His mouth. Consider now what serious answer you are to make for yourself and your party; our cause, supported as it is by the truth of God, will be at no loss for a complete defense. I speak not of our persons, whose safety will be found not in defense, but in humble confession and suppliant petition; but insofar as our ministry is concerned, there is none of us who will not be able to speak for himself as follows.

Defense of His Ministry

"O Lord, I have indeed experienced how difficult and grievous it is to bear the invidious accusations with which I was harassed on the earth; but with the same confidence with which I then appealed to Your tribunal, I now appear before You, for I know that in Your judgment truth reigns. Supported by confidence in this truth, I first dared to attempt, and assisted by it I was able to accomplish, whatever was achieved by me in Your church. They charged me with two of the worst of crimes, heresy and schism. The heresy was that I dared to protest against dogmas received by them.

"But what could I have done? I heard from Your mouth that there was no other light of truth which could direct our souls into the way of life than that which was kindled by Your word. I heard that whatever human minds of themselves conceive concerning Your majesty, the worship of Your deity, and the mysteries of Your religion was vanity. I heard that their introduction into the church of doctrines sprung from the human brain in place of Your word was sacrilegious presumption. But when I turned my eyes toward the people, I saw very different principles prevailing. Those who were regarded as the leaders of faith neither understood Your word, nor greatly cared for it. They only drove unhappy people about with strange doctrines and deluded them with I know not what follies. Among the people themselves, the highest veneration paid to Your word was to revere it at a distance as something inaccessible and to abstain from all investigation of it.

"Owing to the supine dullness of the pastors and the stupidity of the people, every place was filled with pernicious errors, falsehoods, and superstition. They indeed called You the only God, but they did so while transferring to others the glory which You claimed for Your majesty. They imagined for themselves and esteemed as many gods as they had saints to worship. Your Christ was indeed worshiped as God and retained the name of Savior, but where He ought to have been honored, He was left almost destitute of glory. For, spoiled of His own virtue, He passed unnoticed among the crowd of saints, like one of the meanest of them. There was no one who duly considered that one sacrifice which He offered to You on the cross and by which He reconciled us to Yourself; no one who ever dreamed of thinking of His eternal priesthood and the intercession depending on it; no one who trusted in His righteousness only. That confident hope of salvation, which is both enjoined by Your word and founded upon it, had almost vanished. Indeed, it was received as a kind of oracle; it was foolish arrogance and, as they said, presumption for anyone to trust in Your goodness and the righteousness of Your Son and entertain a sure and unfaltering hope of salvation. These were so many profane opinions which, though they were the first principles of that doctrine which You delivered to us in Your word, they plucked up by the roots.

"The true meaning of baptism and the Lord's Supper also was corrupted by numerous falsehoods. And then, when everybody, gravely affronting Your mercy, put confidence in good works, when by good works they strove to merit Your favor, to procure justification, to expiate their sins, and make satisfaction to You (each of these things obliterating and emptying the virtue of Christ's cross), they were yet quite ignorant in what good works consisted. For just as if they were not at all instructed in righteousness by Your law, they had fabricated for themselves many useless trivialities as a means of procuring Your favor, and on these they

so prided themselves that in comparison with them they almost
scorned the standard of true righteousness which Your law commended: to such a degree had human desires usurped the as-
cendancy and derogated, if not from the belief, at least from the
authority of Your precepts contained in it.

"That I might perceive these things, You, O Lord, shone upon
me with the brightness of Your Spirit; that I might comprehend
how impious and harmful they were, You bore before me the
torch of Your word; that I might abominate them as they deserved, You disturbed my soul. But in rendering an account of
my doctrine, You see what my own conscience declares, that it
was not my intention to stray beyond those limits which I saw
had been fixed for all Your servants. Whatever I did not doubt I
had learned from Your mouth I desired to dispense faithfully to
the church. Assuredly the thing at which I chiefly aimed, and
for which I most diligently labored, was that the glory of Your
goodness and justice should disperse the mists by which it was
formerly obscured and might shine forth conspicuously, that the
virtue and blessings of Your Christ, all disguises being brushed
aside, might be fully displayed. For I thought it impious to leave
in obscurity things which we were born to ponder and meditate.
Nor did I think that truths whose magnitude no language can
express were to be maliciously or falsely declared. I hesitated not
to dwell at greater length on topics on which the salvation of
my hearers depended. For the oracle could never deceive which
declares: 'This is eternal life, to know You, the only true God, and
Jesus Christ, whom You have sent' [John 17:3].

"As to the charge of forsaking the church, which they are accustomed to bring against me, there is nothing here of which my conscience accuses me, unless indeed he is to be considered a deserter who, seeing the soldiers routed and scattered and abandoning the ranks, raises the leader's standard and recalls them to their posts. For thus, O Lord, were all Your servants dispersed, so that they could not by any possibility hear the command, but had almost forgotten their leader, their service, and their military vow. To bring them together when thus scattered, I raised not a foreign standard, but that noble banner of Yours which we must follow if we would be classed among Your people.

"Then I was assailed by those who, when they ought to have kept others in their ranks, had led them astray, and when I would not at all desist, they opposed me with violence. On this grievous tumults arose, and the contest flared up into disruption. Who was to blame it is for You, O Lord, to decide. Always, both by word and deed, have I protested how eager I was for unity. Mine, however, was a unity of the church which should begin with You and end in You. For whenever You recommended to us peace and concord, at the same time You showed Yourself to be the only bond for preserving it. But if I desired to be at peace with those who boasted of being the heads of the church and the pillars of faith, I had to purchase it with the denial of Your truth. I thought that anything was to be endured rather than stoop to such an execrable accommodation. For Your Christ Himself declared that, though heaven and earth should be confounded, yet Your word must endure for ever [Matt. 24:35].

"Nor did I think that I dissented from Your church, because I was at war with those leaders. For You forewarned us both by Your Son and by the apostles that into that place there would rise persons to whom I ought by no means to consent. Christ predicted not of strangers, but of those who should pass themselves off as pastors, that they would be ravenous wolves and false prophets, and at the same time warned us to beware of them [Matt. 7:15]. Where Christ ordered me to beware was I to lend my aid? And the apostles declared that there would be no enemies of Your church more pestilential than those from within, who should conceal themselves under the title of pastors [Acts 20:29–30; 2 Pet. 2:1; 1 John 2:18]. Why should I have hesitated to separate myself from persons whom they forewarned me to hold as enemies?

"I had before my eyes the examples of Your prophets who, I saw, had a similar contest with the priests and prophets of their day, though these were undoubtedly the rulers of the church among the Israelite people. But Your prophets are not regarded as schismatics because, when they wished to revive religion which had fallen into decay, they did not desist although opposed with the utmost violence. They still remained in the unity of the church, though they were execrated with awful curses by wicked priests and thought unworthy of a place among people, not to say saints. Confirmed by their example, I too persisted. Though denounced as a deserter of the church and threatened, I was in no respect deterred or induced to proceed less firmly and boldly in opposing those who, in the character of pastors, wasted Your church more than any impious tyranny. My conscience told me how strong the zeal was with which I burned for the unity of Your church, provided Your truth were made the bond of concord. As the tumults which followed were not excited by me, so there is no ground for imputing them to me.

"O Lord, You know, and the fact has testified itself to others, that the only thing I asked was that all controversies should be decided by Your word, that thus both parties might unite with one mind to establish Your kingdom; and I declined not to restore peace to the church at the expense of my head, if I were found to be the cause of needless disturbance. But what did our opponents do? Did they not forthwith furiously fly to fires, swords, and gibbets? Did they not decide that their only security was in arms and cruelty? Did they not instigate all ranks to the same fury? Did they not spurn all methods of pacification? Thus it happens that a matter which might at one time have been settled amicably has blazed up into such a conflict. But although amid the great confusion human judgments were various, I am freed from all fear now that we stand at Your tribunal, where equity combined with truth cannot but decide in favor of innocence."

This, Sadoleto, is our plea, not the fictitious one which you, in order to aggravate our case, were pleased to devise, but one whose perfect truth is known to the good even now and will be made manifest to all creatures on that day. Nor will those who, instructed by our preaching, have come over to our cause be at a loss what to say for themselves, since each will have ready a defense like this.

Defense of a (Protestant) Believer for Breaking with Rome

"I, O Lord, as I had been educated from childhood, always professed the Christian faith. But at first I had no other reason for my faith than that which at the time everywhere prevailed. Your word, which ought to have shone on all Your people like a lamp, was for us taken away or at least suppressed. Lest anyone should long for greater light, an idea had been planted in the minds of all that the investigation of that hidden celestial philosophy was better delegated to a few, whom the others might consult as oracles; for plebeian minds no higher knowledge was proper than to submit themselves to obedience to the church. Now the rudiments in which I had been instructed were of a kind which could neither properly train me to the right worship of Your divinity, nor pave my way to a sure hope of salvation, nor train me aright for the duties of a Christian life. I had learned indeed to worship You alone as my God, but, as the true method of worshiping was altogether unknown to me, I stumbled at the very threshold.

"I believed, as I had been taught, that I was redeemed by the death of Your Son from liability to eternal death, but the redemption I thought of was one whose virtue could never reach me. I expected a future day of resurrection, but hated to think of it, as a most dreadful event. This feeling not only had dominion over me in private, but was derived from the doctrine which was then uniformly delivered to Christian people by their teachers. They indeed preached of Your clemency, but only toward those people who should show themselves worthy. Moreover they put

this value on the righteousness of works, that only he was received into Your favor who reconciled himself to You by works.
At the same time they did not disguise the fact that we are miserable sinners, that we often fall through infirmity of the flesh,
and that to all, therefore, Your mercy must be the common haven
of salvation. But the method of obtaining it which they pointed
out was by making satisfaction to You for offenses. Then satisfaction was enjoined upon us: first, that after confessing all our
sins to a priest, we suppliantly ask pardon and absolution; and
second, that by good deeds we efface from Your remembrance
our bad [ones]; last, that in order to supply what was still wanting, we add sacrifices and solemn expiations. Then, because You
are a stern judge and strict avenger of iniquity, they showed how
dreadful Your presence must be. Hence they bade us flee first to
the saints, that by their intercession You might be easily entreated
and made propitious toward us.

"When, however, I had performed all these things, though I
had some intervals of quiet, I was still far from true peace of
conscience. For whenever I descended into myself or raised my
mind to You, extreme terror seized me which no expiations or
satisfactions could cure. The more closely I examined myself, the
sharper the stings with which my conscience was pricked, so
that the only solace which remained was to delude myself by
obliviousness. Yet as nothing better offered, I was pursuing the
course which I had begun, when a very different form of doctrine started up, not one which led us away from the Christian
profession, but one which brought it back to its source and, as

it were, clearing away the dregs, restored it to its original purity. Offended by the novelty, I lent an unwilling ear and at first, I confess, strenuously and passionately resisted. Such is the firmness or effrontery with which people naturally persist in the course they have once undertaken, that it was with the greatest difficulty I was induced to confess that I had all my life long been in ignorance and error.

"One thing in particular made me averse to those new teachers, namely, reverence for the church. But when once I opened my ears and allowed myself to be taught, I perceived that this fear of derogating from the majesty of the church was groundless. For they reminded me how great the difference is between schism from the church and studying to correct the faults by which the church herself is contaminated. They spoke nobly of the church and showed the greatest desire to cultivate unity. Lest it should seem they quibbled on the term 'church,' they showed it was no new thing for Antichrists to preside there in place of pastors. Of this they produced several examples, from which it appeared that they aimed at nothing but the edification of the church and in that respect made common cause with many of Christ's servants whom we ourselves included in the catalogue of saints. For, attacking more freely the Roman pontiff, who was reverenced as the vicegerent of Christ, the successor of Peter, and the head of the church, they excused themselves thus: such titles as these are empty bugbears, by which the eyes of the pious ought not to be so blinded as not to venture to investigate and sift out the reality. It was when the world was plunged in ignorance and weakness as in a deep sleep that the pope had risen to such an eminence, certainly neither appointed head of the church by the word of God, nor ordained by a legitimate act of the church, but of his own accord and self-elected. Moreover the tyranny which he let loose against the people of God was not to be endured, if we wished to have the kingdom of Christ among us in safety.

"Nor did they lack very powerful arguments to confirm all their positions. First, they clearly disposed of everything that was then commonly adduced to establish the primacy of the pope. When they had taken away all these supports, they also by the word of God tumbled him from his lofty height. As far as the matter allowed, they made it clear and palpable to learned and unlearned that the true order of the church had then perished; that the power of the keys under which the discipline of the church is comprehended had been seriously perverted; that Christian liberty had collapsed; in short, that the kingdom of Christ was prostrated when this primacy was erected. They told me, moreover, as a means of pricking my conscience, that I could not safely connive at these things as if they were no concern of mine; that so far are You from patronizing any voluntary error that even he who is led astray by mere ignorance does not err with impunity. This they proved by the testimony of Your Son: 'If the blind lead the blind, both shall fall into the ditch' [Matt. 15:14].

"My mind was now prepared for serious attention, and I at length perceived, as if light had broken in upon me, in what a dunghill of error I had wallowed and how much pollution and impurity I had thereby contracted. Being exceedingly alarmed at the misery into which I had fallen, and much more at that which threatened me in eternal death, as in duty bound I made it my first business to condemn my own past life, not without groans and tears, and to accept Your life. And now, O Lord, what is left for a wretch like me but, instead of defense, earnestly to supplicate You not to judge according to its deserts that fearful abandonment of Your word, from which in Your wondrous goodness You have at last delivered me."

2. A Letter Regarding His Call to Return to Geneva

This letter to William Farel, one of his closest friends, who had shared exile from Geneva with him in 1538, expresses some of Calvin's thoughts when he felt compelled to return to that city. Central themes are voiced in his words "when I remember that I am not my own, I offer up my heart, presented as a sacrifice to the Lord" and his sense "that it is God with whom I have to do." Here he also indicates his conviction that God can and does direct believers through other human beings. This and all following letters come from Jules Bonnet's collection translated by Marcus Robert Gilchrist. —E. A. McKee

To Farel:

Strasbourg, October 1540

When your letter was brought to me, mine was already written; and although you will find that it does not agree in all points to what you require of me [i.e., to return to Geneva], I have thought it best to forward it to you, that you may be aware what my feelings were at the time when it arrived. Now, however, after I have seen you press the matter further, and that our former guests associate openly in the same cause, I have again had recourse to our magistracy. Having read over your letter and those of the Genevese, I asked what in their opinion was now to be done. They answered that there could be no doubt that, without calling any previous meeting, I ought immediately to set out thither; for the question was not now open or doubt-

ful, although it had not been formally settled. Therefore
we prepare to start on the journey. In order, however,
that the present need of that church may be provided
for, which we are not willing should continue destitute
[until I (Calvin) can come], they are of opinion that Viret
should by all means be sent for thither, in the meantime,
while I am for the present distracted by another charge [in
Strasbourg and the colloquies]. When we come back, our
friends here will not refuse their consent to my return to
Geneva. Moreover, Bucer has pledged himself that he will
accompany me. I have written to them to that effect; and
in order to make the promise all the more certain, Bucer
has accompanied my letter by one from himself.

As to my intended course of proceeding, this is my
present feeling: had I the choice at my own disposal, nothing would be less agreeable to me than to follow your advice. But when I remember that I am not my own, I offer
up my heart, presented as a sacrifice to the Lord. Therefore
there is no ground for your apprehension that you will
only get fine words. Our friends are in earnest and promise sincerely. And for myself, I protest that I have no other
desire than that, setting aside all consideration of me, they
may look only to what is most for the glory of God and
the advantage of the church. Although I am not very in-
genious, I would not lack pretexts by which I might
adroitly slip away, so that I should easily excuse myself in
human sight. I am well aware, however, that it is God with
whom I have to do, from whose sight such crafty imagina-
tions cannot be withheld. Therefore I submit my will and

my affections, subdued and held fast, to the obedience of God; and whenever I am at a loss for counsel of my own, I submit myself to those by whom I hope that the Lord Himself will speak to me.

When Capito wrote, he supposed, as I perceive, that I would, in a lengthy and tiresome narrative, relate to you the whole course of our deliberation; but it is enough that you have the sum of it; although I would have done that also had there been time. But the whole day was taken up in various avocations. Now, after supper, I am not much inclined by sitting up longer to trifle with my health, which is at best in a doubtful state. This messenger has promised to return here at Christmas with the carriage, in which he can bring along with him to Wendelin, of the books which belong to him, ten copies of the Institution, six of [Oecolampadius's] Commentaries on Jeremiah: these you will give to be brought away with him.

[Calvin]

3. Letters About His Wife's Death

Calvin has often been pictured as a very cold man. The letters about the death of his wife, Idelette de Bure, written to two of his closest friends, reveal a man of deep feeling who was convinced that the highest praise he could give her was to honor their shared devotion to God; he regarded his wife as "the best companion of my life" and one who shared his work as "the faithful helper of my ministry."

—E. A. McKee

To Farel:

Geneva, 2 April 1549

Intelligence of my wife's death has perhaps reached you before now. I do what I can to keep myself from being overwhelmed with grief. My friends also leave nothing undone that may administer relief to my mental suffering. When your brother left, her life was all but despaired of.

When the brethren were assembled on Tuesday, they thought it best that we should join together in prayer. This was done. When Abel [Poupin] in the name of the rest exhorted her to faith and patience, she briefly (for she was now greatly worn) stated her frame of mind. I afterward added an exhortation which seemed to me appropriate to the occasion. And then, as she had made no allusion to her children, I (fearing that restrained by modesty she might be feeling an anxiety concerning them which would cause her greater suffering than the disease itself) declared in the presence of the brethren that I should henceforth care for them as if they were my own. She replied, "I have already committed them to the Lord." When I replied that that was not to hinder me from doing my part, she immediately answered, "If the Lord shall care for them, I know they will be commended to you." Her magnanimity was so great that she seemed to have already left the world.

About the sixth hour of the day on which she yielded up her soul to the Lord, our brother Bourgoing addressed some pious words to her, and while he was doing so she spoke aloud so that all saw that her heart was raised far above the world. For these were her words: "O glorious resurrection! O God of Abraham and of all our fathers, in You have the faithful trusted during so many past ages, and none of them have trusted in vain. I also will hope." These short sentences were rather ejaculated than distinctly spoken. This did not come from the suggestion of others but from her own reflections, so that she made it obvious in few words what were her own meditations. I had to go out at six o'clock. Having been removed to another apartment after seven, she immediately began to decline. When she felt her voice suddenly failing her, she said: "Let us pray, let us pray. All pray for me." I had now returned. She was unable to speak, and her mind seemed to be troubled. I, having spoken a few words about the love of Christ, the hope of eternal life, concerning our married life and her departure, engaged in prayer. In full possession of her mind, she both heard the prayer and attended to it. Before eight she expired, so calmly that those present could scarcely distinguish between her life and her death.

I at present control my sorrow so that my duties may not be interfered with. But in the meanwhile the Lord has sent other trials upon me.

Adieu, brother and very excellent friend. May the Lord Jesus strengthen you by His Spirit; and may He support me also under this heavy affliction, which would certainly have overcome me, had not He who raises up the prostrate, strengthens the weak, and refreshes the weary stretched forth His hand from heaven to me. Salute all the brethren and your whole family.

Yours,

John Calvin

To Viret:

Geneva, 7 April 1549

Although the death of my wife has been exceedingly painful to me, yet I subdue my grief as well as I can. Friends also are earnest in their duty to me. I confess that they profit me and themselves less than could be wished, yet I can scarcely say how much I am supported by their attentions. But you know well enough how tender, or rather soft, my mind is. Had not a powerful self-control, therefore, been vouchsafed to me, I could not have borne up so long.

And truly mine is no common source of grief. I have been bereaved of the best companion of my life, of one who, if anything more difficult had befallen me, would not only have been the willing sharer of my exile and

indigence, but even of my death. During her life she was
the faithful helper of my ministry. From her I never experienced the slightest hindrance. She was never trouble-
some to me throughout the entire course of her illness;
she was more anxious about her children than about
herself. As I feared these private cares might annoy her to
no purpose, I took occasion, on the third day before her
death, to mention that I would not fail in discharging my
duty to her children. Taking up the matter immediately,
she said, "I have already committed them to God." When I
said that that was not to prevent me from caring for them,
she replied, "I know you will not neglect what you know
has been committed to God." Lately, also, when a certain
woman insisted that she [my wife] should talk with me
regarding these matters, I heard her [my wife] give the
following brief answer: "Assuredly the principal thing is
that they live a pious and holy life. My husband is not to
be urged to instruct them in religious knowledge and in
the fear of God. If they be pious, I am sure he will gladly
be a father to them; but if not, they do not deserve that
I should ask for aught in their behalf." This nobleness of
mind will weigh more with me than a hundred recom-
mendations.

Many thanks for your friendly consolation. Adieu, most
excellent and honest brother. May the Lord Jesus watch
over and direct yourself and your wife. Present my best
wishes to her and to the brethren.

Yours,

John Calvin

4. The Preface to the Commentary on Psalms

*Calvin was always very shy about revealing his personal life
and feelings to any but the closest friends. However, in the
preface to his commentary on Psalms, written relatively late in
his life (1557), the Reformer sketched the fullest outline of his
education and conversion, his ministry and personal struggles
to be found anywhere in his writings. It is significant that
he does this in the context of introducing the book of Psalms,
which he calls "an anatomy of all the parts of the soul" and in
which he demonstrates clearly that emotion is an important
element in human life. The Psalms provide believers with the
best vocabulary of prayer. Strange as it may sound, Calvin felt
a deep affinity with David; though he never claimed to reach
David's heights, Calvin recognized that they shared a similar
struggle in leading the church, and he modeled his own prayer
life on that of the Old Testament psalm singer. The translation
is by James Anderson.*

—E. A. McKee

If the reading of these my commentaries confers as much benefit
on the church of God as I myself have reaped advantage from the
composition of them, I shall have no reason to regret that I have
undertaken this work....

The varied and resplendent riches which are contained in this
treasury it is no easy matter to express in words; so much so, that
I well know that whatever I shall be able to say will be far from

approaching the excellence of the subject. But as it is better to give to my readers some taste, however small, of the wonderful advantages they will derive from the study of this book than to be entirely silent on the point, I may be permitted briefly to advert to a matter the greatness of which does not admit of being fully unfolded. I have been accustomed to call this book, I think not inappropriately, "An Anatomy of All the Parts of the Soul"; for there is not an emotion of which anyone can be conscious that is not here represented as in a mirror. Or, rather, the Holy Spirit has here drawn to life all the griefs, sorrows, fears, doubts, hopes, cares, perplexities, in short, all the distracting emotions with which human minds are wont to be agitated. The other parts of Scripture contain the commandments which God enjoined His servants to announce to us. But here the prophets themselves, seeing they are exhibited to us as speaking to God and laying open all their inmost thoughts and affections, call, or rather draw, each of us to the examination of himself in particular, in order that none of the many infirmities to which we are subject and of the many vices with which we abound may remain concealed. It is certainly a rare and singular advantage when all lurking places are discovered and the heart is brought into the light, purged from that most baneful infection, hypocrisy.

In short, as calling upon God is one of the principal means of securing our safety, and as a better and more unerring rule for guiding us in this exercise cannot be found elsewhere than in the Psalms, it follows that in proportion to the proficiency which a person shall have attained in understanding them will be his knowledge of the most important part of celestial doctrine. Genuine and earnest prayer proceeds, first, from a sense of our need and, next, from faith in the promises of God. It is by perusing these inspired compositions that people will be most effectually awakened to a sense of their maladies and, at the same time, instructed in seeking remedies for their cure. In a word, whatever may serve to encourage us when we are about to pray to God is taught us in this book. And not only are the promises of God presented to us in it, but oftentimes there is exhibited to us one standing, as it were, amidst the invitations of God on the one hand and the impediments of the flesh on the other, girding and preparing himself for prayer: thus teaching us, if at any time we are agitated with a variety of doubts, to resist and fight against them until the soul, freed and disentangled from all these impediments, rises up to God; and not only so, but even when in the midst of doubts, fears, and apprehensions, let us put forth our efforts in prayer until we experience some consolation which may calm and bring contentment to our minds.

Although distrust may shut the gate against our prayers, yet we must not allow ourselves to give way whenever our hearts waver or are agitated with inquietude, but must persevere until faith finally comes forth victorious from these conflicts. In many places we may perceive the exercise of the servants of God in prayer so fluctuating that they are almost overwhelmed by the alternate hope of success and apprehension of failure and gain the prize only by strenuous exertions. We see, on the one hand, the flesh manifesting its infirmity and, on the other, faith putting forth its power; and if it is not so valiant and courageous as might be desired, it is at least prepared to fight until by degrees it acquires perfect strength.

But as those things which serve to teach us the true method of praying aright will be found scattered through the whole of this commentary, I will not now stop to treat of topics which it will be necessary afterward to repeat, not detain my readers from proceeding to the work itself. Only it appeared to me to be requisite to show in passing that this book makes known to us this privilege which is desirable above all others—that not only is there opened up to us familiar access to God, but also that we have permission and freedom granted us to lay open before Him our infirmities which we would be ashamed to confess before other people.

Besides, there is also here prescribed to us an infallible rule for directing us with respect to the right manner of offering to God the sacrifice of praise, which He declares to be most precious in His sight and of the sweetest odor. There is no other book in which there are to be found more express and magnificent commendations, both of the unparalleled liberality of God toward His church and of all His works; there is no other book in which there are recorded so many deliverances, or one in which the evidences and experiences of the fatherly providence and solicitude which God exercises toward us are celebrated with such splendor of diction and yet with the strictest adherence to truth; in short, there is no other book in which we are more perfectly taught the right manner of praising God, or in which we are more powerfully stirred up to the performance of this exercise of piety.

Moreover, although the Psalms are replete with all the precepts which serve to frame our life to every part of holiness, piety, and righteousness, yet they will principally teach and train us to bear the cross; and the bearing of the cross is a genuine proof of our obedience, since by doing this we renounce the guidance of our own affections and submit ourselves entirely to God, leaving Him to govern us and to dispose of our life according to His will, so that the afflictions which are the bitterest and most severe to our nature become sweet to us because they proceed from Him. In one word, not only will we here find general commendations of the goodness of God which may teach people to repose themselves in Him alone and to seek all their happiness solely in Him, and which are intended to teach devout believers with their whole hearts confidently to look to Him for help in all their necessities; but we will also find that the free remission of sins, which alone reconciles God toward us and procures for us settled peace with Him, is so set forth and magnified as that here there is nothing wanting which relates to the knowledge of eternal salvation.

Now, if my readers derive any fruit and advantage from the labor which I have bestowed in writing these commentaries, I would have them to understand that the small measure of experience which I have had by the conflicts with which the Lord has exercised me has in no ordinary degree assisted me, not only in applying to present use whatever instruction could be gathered from these divine compositions, but also in more easily comprehending the design of each of the writers. And as David holds the

principal place among them, it has greatly aided me in understanding more fully the complaints made by him of the internal
afflictions which the church had to sustain through those who
gave themselves out to be her members, that I had suffered the
same or similar things from the domestic enemies of the church.
For although I follow David at a great distance and come far short
of equaling him; or rather, although in aspiring slowly and with
great difficulty to attain to the many virtues in which he excelled,
I still feel myself tarnished with the contrary vices; yet if I have
any things in common with him, I have no hesitation in compar-
ing myself with him.

In reading the instances of his faith, patience, fervor, zeal, and
integrity, it has (as it ought) drawn from me unnumbered groans
and sighs that I am so far from approaching them; but it has
notwithstanding been of very great advantage to me to behold in
him as in a mirror both the commencement of my calling and
the continued course of my function, so that I know the more
assuredly that whatever that most illustrious king and prophet
suffered was exhibited to me by God as an example for imitation. My condition no doubt is much inferior to his, and it is
unnecessary for me to stay to show this. But as he was taken from
the sheepfold and elevated to the rank of supreme authority, so
God, having taken me from my originally obscure and humble
condition, has reckoned me worthy of being invested with the
honorable office of a preacher and minister of the gospel.

When I was as yet a very little boy, my father had destined me
for the study of theology. But afterward, when he considered that
the legal profession commonly raised those who followed it to

wealth, this prospect induced him suddenly to change his purpose. Thus it came to pass that I was withdrawn from the study of philosophy and was put to the study of law. To this pursuit I endeavored faithfully to apply myself, in obedience to the will of my father; but God, by the secret guidance of His providence, at length gave a different direction to my course. And first, since I was too obstinately devoted to the superstitions of Popery to be easily extricated from so profound an abyss of mire, God by a sudden conversion subdued and brought to a teachable frame my mind, which was more hardened in such matters than might have been expected from one at my early period of life. Having thus received some taste and knowledge of true piety, I was immediately inflamed with so intense a desire to make progress therein that, although I did not altogether leave off other studies, I yet pursued them with less ardor.

I was quite surprised to find that before a year had elapsed, all who had any desire for purer doctrine were continually coming to me to learn, although I myself was as yet but a mere novice and tyro. Being of a disposition somewhat unpolished and bashful, which led me always to love the shade and retirement, I then began to seek some secluded corner where I might be withdrawn from the public view; but so far from being able to accomplish the object of my desire, all my retreats were like public schools. In short, although my one great object was to live in seclusion without being known, God so led me about through different turnings and changes that He never permitted me to rest in any place until, in spite of my natural disposition, He brought me forth to public notice.

Leaving my native county, France, I in fact retired into Germany expressly for the purpose of being able there to enjoy in some obscure corner the repose which I had always desired and which had been so long denied me. But lo! while I lay hidden at Basel and known only to a few people, many faithful and holy persons were burned alive in France; and the report of these burnings having reached foreign nations, they excited the strongest disapprobation among a great part of the Germans, whose indignation was kindled against the authors of such tyranny. In order to allay this indignation, certain wicked and lying pamphlets were circulated stating that none were treated with such cruelty but Anabaptists and seditious persons, who by their perverse ravings and false opinions were overthrowing not only religion but also all civil order. Observing that the object which these instruments of the court aimed at by their disguises was not only that the disgrace of shedding so much innocent blood might remain buried under the false charges and calumnies which they brought against the holy martyrs after their death, but also that afterward they might be able to proceed to the utmost extremity in murdering the poor saints without exciting compassion toward them in the breasts of any, it appeared to me that, unless I opposed them to the utmost of my ability, my silence could not be vindicated from the charge of cowardice and treachery.

This was the consideration which induced me to publish my *Institutes of the Christian Religion.* My objects were, first, to prove that these reports were false and calumnious and thus to vindicate my brethren, whose death was precious in the sight of the Lord; and next, that as the same cruelties might very soon after be exercised against many unhappy individuals, foreign nations might be touched with at least some compassion toward them and solicitude about them. When it was then published, it was not that copious and labored work which it now is, but only a small treatise containing a summary of the principal truths of the Christian religion; and it was published with no other design than that the peoples might know what faith was held by those whom I saw basely and wickedly defamed by those flagitious and perfidious flatterers. That my object was not to acquire fame appeared from this, that immediately afterward I left Basel, and particularly from the fact that nobody there knew that I was the author.

Wherever else I have gone, I have taken care to conceal that I was the author of that performance; and I had resolved to continue in the same privacy and obscurity until at length William Farel detained me at Geneva, not so much by counsel and exhortation as by a dreadful imprecation, which I felt to be as if God had from heaven laid His mighty hand upon me to arrest me. As the most direct road to Strasbourg, to which I then intended to retire, was shut up by the wars, I had resolved to pass quickly by Geneva without staying longer than a single night in that city. A little before this, Popery had been driven from it by the exertions of the excellent person whom I have named and Peter Viret; but matters were not yet brought to a settled state, and the city was divided into unholy and dangerous factions.

Then an individual who has now basely apostatized and returned to the papists discovered me and made me known to others. Upon this, Farel, who burned with an extraordinary zeal to advance the gospel, immediately strained every nerve to detain me. And after having learned that my heart was set upon devoting myself to private studies, for which I wished to keep myself free from other pursuits, and finding that he gained nothing by entreaties, he proceeded to utter an imprecation that God would curse my retirement and the tranquility of the studies which I sought, if I should withdraw and refuse to give assistance when the necessity was so urgent. By this imprecation I was so stricken with terror that I desisted from the journey which I had undertaken; but sensible of my natural bashfulness and timidity, I would not bring myself under obligation to discharge any particular office.

After that, four months had scarcely elapsed, when, on the one hand, the Anabaptists began to assail us and, on the other, a certain wicked apostate who, being secretly supported by the influence of some of the magistrates of the city, was thus enabled to give us a great deal of trouble. At the same time, a succession of dissensions fell out in the city which strangely afflicted us. Being, as I acknowledge, naturally of a timid, soft, and pusillanimous disposition, I was compelled to encounter these violent tempests as part of my early training; and although I did not sink under them, yet I was not sustained by such greatness of mind as not to rejoice more than it became me when in consequence of certain commotions I was banished from Geneva.

By this means set at liberty and loosed from the tie of my vocation, I resolved to live in a private station, free from the burden and cares of any public charge, when that most excellent servant of Christ, Martin Bucer, employing a similar kind of remonstrance and protestation as that to which Farel had recourse before, drew me back to a new station. Alarmed by the example of Jonah which he set before me, I still continued in the work of teaching. And although I always continued like myself, studiously avoiding celebrity, yet I was carried, I know not how, as it were by force to the Imperial assemblies, where, willing or unwilling, I was under the necessity of appearing before the eyes of many. Afterward, when the Lord, having compassion on this city, had allayed the hurtful agitations and broils which prevailed in it and by His wonderful power had defeated both the wicked counsels and the sanguinary attempts of the disturbers of the Republic, necessity was imposed upon me of returning to my former charge, contrary to my desire and inclination. The welfare of this church, it is true, lay so near my heart that for its sake I would not have hesitated to lay down my life; but my timidity nevertheless suggested to me many reasons for excusing myself from again willingly taking upon my shoulders so heavy a burden. At length, however, a solemn and conscientious regard for my duty prevailed with me to consent to return to the flock from which I had been torn; but with what grief, tears, great anxiety, and distress I did this the Lord is my best witness, and many godly persons who would have wished to see me delivered from this painful state, had it not been that that which I feared, and which made me give my consent, prevented them and shut their mouths.

Were I to narrate the various conflicts by which the Lord has exercised me since that time and by what trials He has proved me, it would make a long history. But that I may not become tedious to my readers by a waste of words, I shall content myself with repeating briefly what I touched upon a little before, that in considering the whole course of the life of David it seemed to me that by his own footsteps he showed me the way, and from this I have experienced no small consolation. As that holy king was harassed by the Philistines and other foreign enemies with continual wars, while he was much more grievously afflicted by the malice and wickedness of some perfidious ones among his own people, so I can say, as to myself, that I have been assailed on all sides and have scarcely been able to enjoy repose for a single moment, but have always had to sustain some conflict either from enemies without or within the church.... This knowledge and experience have been of much service in enabling me to understand the Psalms, so that in my meditations upon them I did not wander, as it were, in an unknown region.

My readers too, if I mistake not, will observe that in unfolding the internal affections both of David and of others I discourse upon them as matters of which I have familiar experience. Moreover, since I have labored faithfully to open up this treasure for the use of all the people of God, although what I have done has not been equal to my wishes, yet the attempt which I have made deserves to be received with some measure of favor. Still, I only ask that each may judge of my labors with justice and candor, according to the advantage and fruit which he shall derive from them.... I have felt nothing to be of more importance than to have a regard to the edification of the church. May God, who has implanted this desire in my heart, grant by His grace that the success may correspond thereto!

II. THEOLOGY AND SCRIPTURE

5. Piety

The Institutes of the Christian Religion *is Calvin's
comprehensive, coherent statement of biblical and creedal faith.
This selection is from Book One,* The Knowledge of God
the Creator, *which outlines the human condition before
God and the knowledge of God and ourselves, thus delineating
Calvin's first definition of piety. All excerpts from the Institutes are translated by F. L. Battles.*

—E. A. McKee

The Knowledge of God and That of Ourselves Are Connected

Nearly all the wisdom we possess, that is to say, true and sound
wisdom, consists of two parts: the knowledge of God and of ourselves. But, although joined by many bonds, which one precedes
and brings forth the other is not easy to discern. In the first place,
no one can look upon himself without immediately turning his
thoughts to the contemplation of God, in whom he "lives and
moves." For, quite clearly, the mighty gifts with which we are endowed are hardly from ourselves; indeed, our very being is nothing but subsistence in the one God. Then, by these benefits shed
like dew from heaven upon us, we are led as by rivulets to the
spring itself. Indeed, our very poverty better discloses the infini-
tude of benefits reposing in God. The miserable ruin into which
the rebellion of the first human being cast us especially compels us
to look upward. Thus, not only may we in fasting and hungering

seek thence what we lack; but, in being aroused by fear, we may learn humility. For, as a veritable world of miseries is to be found in the human race and we are thereby despoiled of divine raiment, our shameful nakedness exposes a teeming horde of infamies.

Each of us must, then, be so stung by the consciousness of his own unhappiness as to attain at least some knowledge of God. Thus, from the feeling of our own ignorance, vanity, poverty, infirmity, and—what is more—depravity and corruption, we recognize that the true light of wisdom, sound virtue, full abundance of every good, and purity of righteousness rest in the Lord alone. To this extent we are prompted by our own ills to contemplate the good things of God; and we cannot seriously aspire to Him before we begin to become displeased with ourselves. For what person in all the world would not gladly remain as he is—what one does not remain as he is—so long as he does not know himself, that is, while content with his own gifts and either ignorant or unmindful of his own misery? Accordingly, the knowledge of ourselves not only arouses us to seek God, but also, as it were, leads us by the hand to find Him.

Again, it is certain that a person never achieves a clear knowledge of himself unless he has first looked upon God's face and then descends from contemplating God to scrutinize himself. For we always seem to ourselves righteous and upright and wise and holy—this pride is innate in all of us—unless by clear proofs we stand convinced of our own unrighteousness, foulness, folly, and impurity. Moreover, we are not thus convinced if we look merely to ourselves and not also to the Lord, who is the sole standard by which this judgment must be measured. For, because all of us are inclined by nature to hypocrisy, a kind of empty image of righteousness in place of righteousness itself abundantly satisfies us. And because nothing appears within or around us that has not been contaminated by great immorality, what is a little less vile pleases us as a thing most pure—so long as we confine our minds within the limits of human corruption. Just so an eye to which nothing is shown but black objects judges something dirty white or even rather darkly mottled to be whiteness itself.

Indeed, we can discern still more clearly from the bodily senses how much we are deluded in estimating the powers of the soul. For if in broad daylight we either look down upon the ground or survey whatever meets our view round about, we seem to our selves endowed with the strongest and keenest sight; yet when we look up to the sun and gaze straight at it, that power of sight which was particularly strong on earth is at once blunted and confused by a great brilliance, and thus we are compelled to admit that our keenness in looking upon things earthly is sheer dullness when it comes to the sun. So it happens in estimating our spiritual goods. As long as we do not look beyond the earth, being quite content with our own righteousness, wisdom, and virtue, we flatter ourselves most sweetly and fancy ourselves all but demigods. Suppose we but once begin to raise our thoughts to God and to ponder His nature and how completely perfect are His righteousness, wisdom, and power—the straightedge to which we must be shaped. Then, what masquerading earlier as righteousness was pleasing in us will soon grow filthy in its consummate wickedness. What wonderfully impressed us under the name of wisdom will stink in its very foolishness. What wore the face of power will prove itself the most miserable weakness. That is, what in us seems perfection itself corresponds ill to the purity of God.

Hence that dread and wonder with which Scripture commonly represents the saints as stricken and overcome whenever they felt the presence of God. Thus it comes about that we see people who in God's absence normally remained firm and constant, but who, when He manifests His glory, are so shaken and struck dumb as to be laid low by the dread of death—are in fact overwhelmed by it and almost annihilated. As a consequence, we must infer that no one is ever sufficiently touched and affected by the awareness of his lowly state until he has compared himself with God's majesty. Moreover, we have numerous examples of this consternation both in the book of Judges and in the Prophets. So frequent was it that this expression was common among God's people: "We shall die, for the Lord has appeared to us" [Judg. 13:22; Isa. 6:5; Ezek. 2:1]. The story of Job, in its description of God's wisdom, power, and purity, always expresses a most powerful argument that overwhelms people with the realization of their own stupidity, impotence, and corruption. And not without cause: for we see how Abraham recognizes more clearly that he is earth and dust when once he has come nearer to beholding God's glory [Gen. 18:27]; and how Elijah, with uncovered face, cannot bear to await His approach, such is the awesomeness of His appearance [1 Kings 19:13]. And what can a human being do, who is rottenness itself and a worm, when even the very cherubim must veil their faces out of fear? It is this indeed of which the prophet Isaiah speaks: "The sun will blush and the moon be confounded when the Lord of Hosts shall reign" [Isa. 24:23]; that is, when He shall bring forth His splendor and cause it to draw nearer, the brightest thing will become darkness before it.

Yet, however the knowledge of God and of ourselves may be mutually connected, the order of right teaching requires that we discuss the former first, then proceed afterward to treat the latter.

What It Is to Know God

Now the knowledge of God, as I understand it, is that by which we not only conceive that there is a God, but also grasp what befits us to know and is proper to His glory, in fine, what is to our advantage to know of Him. Indeed, we shall not say that, properly speaking, God is known where there is no religion or piety. Here I do not yet touch upon the sort of knowledge with which human beings, in themselves lost and accursed, apprehend God the Redeemer in Christ the Mediator; but I speak only of the primal and simple knowledge to which the very order of nature would have led us if Adam had remained upright. In this ruin of the human race no one now experiences God either as Father or as Author of salvation, or favorable in any way, until Christ the Mediator comes forward to reconcile us to Him. Nevertheless, it is one thing to feel that God as our Maker supports us by His power, governs us by His providence, nourishes us by His goodness, and attends us with all sorts of blessings—and another thing to embrace the grace of reconciliation offered to us in Christ. First, as much in the fashioning of the universe as in the general teaching of Scripture the Lord shows Himself to be simply the Creator. Then in the face of Christ He shows Himself the Redeemer. Of the resulting twofold knowledge of God we shall now discuss the first aspect; the second will be dealt with in its proper place.

Moreover, although our mind cannot apprehend God without rendering some honor to Him, it will not suffice simply to hold that there is One whom all ought to honor and adore, unless we are also persuaded that He is the fountain of every good and that we must seek nothing elsewhere than in Him. This I take to mean that not only does He sustain this universe (as He once founded it) by His boundless might, regulate it by His wisdom, preserve it by His goodness, and especially rule the human race by His righteousness and judgment, bear with it in His mercy, and watch over it by His protection, but also that no drop will be found either of wisdom and light, or of righteousness or power or rectitude, or of genuine truth which does not flow from Him and of which He is not the cause. Thus we may learn to await and seek all these things from Him and thankfully to ascribe them, once received, to Him. For this sense of the powers of God is for us a fit teacher of piety, from which religion is born. I call "piety" that reverence joined with love of God which the knowledge of His benefits induces. For until people recognize that they owe everything to God, that they are nourished by His fatherly care, that He is the Author of their every good, so that they should seek nothing beyond Him—they will never yield Him willing service. Nay, unless they establish their complete happiness in Him, they will never give themselves truly and sincerely to Him.

What is God? Those who pose this question are merely toying with idle speculations. It is more important for us to know of what sort He is and what is consistent with His nature. What good is it to profess with Epicurus some sort of God who has cast aside the care of the world only to amuse Himself in idleness? What help is it, in short, to know a God with whom we have nothing to do? Rather, our knowledge should serve first to teach us fear and reverence; second, with it as our guide and teacher, we should learn to seek every good from Him and, having received it, to credit it to His account. For how can the thought of God penetrate your mind without your realizing immediately that, since you are His handiwork, you have been made over and bound to His command by right of creation, that you owe your life to Him—that whatever you undertake, whatever you do, ought to be ascribed to Him? If this be so, it now assuredly follows that your life is wickedly corrupt unless it be disposed to His service, seeing that His will ought for us to be the law by which we live. Again, you cannot behold Him clearly unless you acknowledge Him to be the fountainhead and source of every good. From this too would arise the desire to cleave to Him and trust in Him, but for the fact that human depravity seduces a person's mind from rightly seeking Him.

For, to begin with, the pious mind does not dream up for itself any god it pleases, but contemplates the one and only true God. And it does not attach to Him whatever it pleases, but is content to hold Him to be as He manifests Himself; furthermore, the mind always exercises the utmost diligence and care not to wander astray or rashly and boldly to go beyond His will. It thus recognizes God, because it knows that He governs all things, and trusts that He is its guide and protector, therefore giving itself over completely to trust in Him. Because it understands Him to be the Author of every good, if anything oppresses, if anything is lacking, immediately it betakes itself to His protection, waiting for help from Him. Because it is persuaded that He is good and merciful, it reposes in Him with perfect trust and doubts not that in His loving-kindness a remedy will be provided for all its ills. Because it acknowledges Him as Lord and Father, the pious mind also deems it meet and right to observe His authority in all things, reverence His majesty, take care to advance His glory, and obey His commandments. Because it sees Him to be a righteous judge, armed with severity to punish wickedness, it ever holds His judgment seat before its gaze and, through fear of Him, restrains itself from provoking His anger.

And yet it is not so terrified by the awareness of His judgment as to wish to withdraw, even if some way of escape were open. But it embraces Him no less as punisher of the wicked than as benefactor of the pious. For the pious mind realizes that the punishment of the impious and wicked and the reward of life eternal for the righteous equally pertain to God's glory. Besides, this mind restrains itself from sinning not out of dread of punishment alone, but because it loves and reveres God as Father, it worships and adores Him as Lord. Even if there were no hell, it would still shudder at only offending Him.

Here indeed is pure and real religion: faith so joined with an earnest fear of God that this fear also embraces willing reverence and carries with it such legitimate worship as is prescribed in the law. And we ought to note this fact even more diligently: all people have a vague general veneration for God, but very few really reverence Him; and wherever there is great ostentation in ceremonies, sincerity of heart is rare indeed.

6. Faith

From the Institutes of the Christian Religion, Book
Three, The Way in Which We Receive the Grace of
Christ. Book Three explains the character of the individual
human relationship with God the Father, the Son, and the Holy
Spirit.

—E. A. McKee

Faith: Its Definition Set Forth, and Its Properties Explained

Now, therefore, we hold faith to be a knowledge of God's will toward us, perceived from His word. But the foundation of this is a preconceived conviction of God's truth.... But since our hearts are not aroused to faith at every word of God, we must find out at this point what, strictly speaking, faith looks to in the word....

It is plain that we do not yet have a full definition of faith, inasmuch as merely to know something of God's will is not to be accounted faith. But what if we were to substitute His benevolence or His mercy in place of His will, the tidings of which are often sad and the proclamation frightening? Thus, surely, we shall more closely approach the nature of faith: for it is after we have learned that our salvation rests with God that we are attracted to seek Him. This fact is confirmed for us when He declares that our salvation is His care and concern. Accordingly, we need the promise of grace, which can testify to us that the Father is merciful, since we can approach Him in no other way, and upon grace alone the human heart can rest.... But we have already seen that the sole pledge of His love is Christ, without whom the signs of hatred and wrath are everywhere evident....

Now we shall possess a right definition of faith if we call it a firm and certain knowledge of God's goodwill toward us, founded upon the truth of the freely given promise in Christ, both revealed to our minds and sealed upon our hearts through the Holy Spirit.

Now let us examine anew the individual parts of the definition of faith. After we have diligently examined it, no doubt, I believe, will remain. When we call faith "knowledge," we do not mean comprehension of the sort that is commonly concerned with those things which fall under human sense perception. Faith is so far above sense that the mind has to go beyond and rise above itself in order to attain it. Even where the mind has attained, it does not comprehend what it feels. But although it is persuaded of what it does not grasp, by the very certainty of its persuasion it understands more than if it perceived anything human by its own capacity.... But [believers] are more strengthened by the persuasion of divine truth than instructed by rational proof.... From this we conclude that the knowledge of faith consists in assurance rather than in comprehension.

Here indeed is the chief hinge on which faith turns: that we do not regard the promises of mercy that God offers as true only outside ourselves, but not at all in us; rather, that we make them ours by inwardly embracing them. Hence, at last is born that confidence which Paul elsewhere calls "peace" [Rom. 5:1]....

When one is stricken by the thought that God is Avenger of

iniquities, faith sets over against this the fact that His pardon is ready for all iniquities whenever the sinner betakes himself to the Lord's mercy. Thus the devout mind, however strange the ways in which it is vexed and troubled, finally surmounts all difficulties and never allows itself to be deprived of assurance of divine mercy....

For not only does piety beget reverence toward God, but the very sweetness and delightfulness of grace so fills one who is cast down in himself with fear, and at the same time with admiration, that he depends upon God and humbly submits himself to His power.

If you contemplate yourself, that is sure damnation. But since Christ has been so imparted to you with all His benefits that all His things are made yours, that you are made a member of Him, indeed one with Him, His righteousness overwhelms your sins: His salvation wipes out your condemnation; with His worthiness He intercedes that your unworthiness may not come before God's sight. Surely this is so: we ought not to separate Christ from ourselves or ourselves from Him. Rather, we ought to hold fast bravely with both hands to that fellowship by which He has bound Himself to us.... Christ is not outside us, but dwells within us. Not only does He cleave to us by an indivisible bond of fellowship, but with a wonderful communion, day by day, He grows more and more into one body with us, until He becomes completely one with us....

We make the freely given promise of God the foundation of faith, because upon it faith properly rests. Faith is certain that God is true in all things whether He commands or forbids, whether He promises or threatens; and it also obediently receives His commandments, observes His prohibitions, heeds His threats. Nevertheless, faith properly begins with the promise, rests in it, and ends in it.... Therefore, when we say that faith must rest upon a freely given promise, we do not deny that believers embrace and grasp the word of God in every respect: but we point out the promise of mercy as the proper goal of faith....

And this bare and external proof of the word of God should have been amply sufficient to engender faith, did not our blindness and perversity prevent it. But our mind has such an inclination to vanity that it can never cleave fast to the truth of God; and it has such a dullness that it is always blind to the light of God's truth. Accordingly, without the illumination of the Holy Spirit, the word can do nothing. From this, also, it is clear that faith is much higher than human understanding. And it will not be enough for the mind to be illumined by the Spirit of God unless the heart is also strengthened and supported by His power....

Indeed, the word of God is like the sun, shining upon all those to whom it is proclaimed, but with no effect among the blind. Now, all of us are blind by nature in this respect. Accordingly, it cannot penetrate into our minds unless the Spirit, as the inner teacher, through His illumination makes entry for it.

It now remains to pour into the heart itself what the mind has absorbed. For the word of God is not received by faith if it flits about in the top of the brain, but when it takes root in the depth of the heart that it may be an invincible defense to withstand and drive off all the stratagems of temptation. But if it is true that the mind's real understanding is illumination by the Spirit of God, then in such confirmation of the heart His power is much more clearly manifested, to the extent that the heart's distrust is greater than the mind's blindness. It is harder for the heart to be furnished with assurance than for the mind to be endowed with thought. The Spirit accordingly serves as a seal, to seal up in our hearts those very promises the certainty of which it has previously impressed upon our minds, and takes the place of a guarantee to confirm and establish them....

Our Regeneration by Faith: Repentance

With good reason, the sum of the gospel is held to consist in repentance and forgiveness of sins.... For since pardon and for-giveness are offered through the preaching of the gospel in or-der that the sinner, freed from the tyranny of Satan, the yoke of sin, and the miserable bondage of vices, may cross over into the kingdom of God, surely no one can embrace the grace of the gospel without betaking himself from the errors of his past life into the right way and applying his whole effort to the practice of repentance....

[No one] can apply himself seriously to repentance without knowing himself to belong to God. But no one is truly persuad-ed that he belongs to God unless he has first recognized God's grace.... Here it is not a question of how variously Christ draws us to Himself or prepares us for the pursuit of piety. I say only that no uprightness can be found except where that Spirit reigns that Christ received to communicate to His members....

Justification by Faith

Christ was given to us by God's generosity, to be grasped and possessed by us in faith. By partaking of Him, we principally receive a double grace: namely, that being reconciled to God through Christ's blamelessness, we may have in heaven instead of a Judge a gracious Father; and second, that sanctified by Christ's Spirit we may cultivate blamelessness and purity of life.... [Justification] is the main hinge on which religion turns, so that we devote the greater attention and care to it. For unless you first of all grasp what your relationship to God is and the nature of His judgment concerning you, you have neither a foundation on which to establish your salvation nor one on which to build piety toward God....

Justified by faith is he who, excluded from the righteousness of works, grasps the righteousness of Christ through faith and, clothed in it, appears in God's sight not as a sinner, but as a righteous person. Therefore we explain justification simply as the acceptance with which God receives us into His favor as righteous. And we say that it consists in the remission of sins and the imputation of Christ's righteousness.

The grace of justification is not separated from regeneration, although they are things distinct. But because it is very well known by experience that the traces of sin always remain in the righteous, their justification must be very different from reformation into newness of life. For God so begins this second point [regeneration] in His elect and progresses in it gradually, and sometimes slowly, throughout life, that they are always liable to the judgment of death before His tribunal. But He does not justify in part but liberally, so that they may appear in heaven as if endowed with the purity of Christ....

7. The Church

From the Institutes of the Christian Religion, *Book Four,* The External Means or Aids by Which God Invites Us into the Society of Christ and Holds Us Therein. *Book Four outlines the external means by which faith is communicated and nourished. Although not restricted to these means, God by accommodation chooses to work through the church, the body of Christ, and Christians are that body as they are engrafted into Christ. Salvation is personal, but not individualistic; Christians are redeemed as members of a body. Preaching and the visible words of the sacraments are God's gifts, delivered by humans, to draw human beings to God.*

—E. A. MCKEE

The True Church with Which We Must Keep Unity

As explained in the previous book, it is by the faith in the gospel that Christ becomes ours and we are made partakers of the salvation and eternal blessedness brought by Him. Since, however, in our ignorance and sloth (to which I add fickleness of disposition) we need outward helps to beget and increase faith within us and advance it to its goal, God has also added these aids that He may provide for our weakness. And in order that the preaching of the gospel might flourish, He deposited this treasure in the church. He instituted "pastors and teachers" [Eph. 4:11] through whose lips He might teach His own; He furnished them with authority;

finally, He omitted nothing that might make for holy agreement of faith and for right order. First of all, He instituted sacraments, which we who have experienced them feel to be highly useful aids to foster and strengthen faith. Shut up as we are in the prison house of our flesh, we have not yet attained angelic rank. God, therefore, in His wonderful providence, accommodating Himself to our capacity, has prescribed a way for us, though still far off, to draw near to Him....

The article in the Creed in which we profess to "believe the church" refers not only to the visible church (our present topic), but also to all God's elect, in whose number are also included the dead.... It is not sufficient for us to comprehend in mind and thought the multitude of the elect, unless we consider the unity of the church as that into which we are convinced we have been engrafted. For no hope of future inheritance remains to us unless we have been united with all other members under Christ, our Head....

The "communion of the saints" ... very well expresses what the church is. It is as if one said that the saints are gathered into the society of Christ on the principle that whatever benefits God confers upon them they should in turn share with one another.... For here we are not bidden to distinguish between reprobate and elect—that is for God alone, not for us, to do—but to establish with certainty in our hearts that all those who, by the kindness of God the Father, through the working of the Holy Spirit, have entered into fellowship with Christ are set apart as God's property and personal possession, and that when we are of their number we share that great grace.

We see how God, who could in a moment perfect His own, nevertheless desires them to grow up into maturity solely under the education of the church. We see the way set for it: the preaching of the heavenly doctrine has been enjoined upon the pastors.... By this plan He willed of old that holy assemblies be held at the sanctuary in order that the doctrine taught by the mouth of the priest might foster agreement in faith.... On the one hand, He proves our obedience by a very good test when we hear His ministers speaking just as if He Himself spoke. On the other, He also provides for our weakness in that He prefers to address us in human fashion through interpreters in order to draw us to Himself, rather than to thunder at us and drive us away.... For, among the many excellent gifts with which God has adorned the human race, it is a singular privilege that He deigns to consecrate to Himself human mouths and tongues in order that His voice may resound in them. Let us accordingly not in turn dislike to embrace obediently the doctrine of salvation put forth by His command and by His own mouth. For, although God's power is not bound to outward means, He has nevertheless bound us to this ordinary manner of teaching.... Believers were bidden of old to seek the face of God in the sanctuary [Ps. 105:1], as is oftentimes repeated in the law, for no other reason than that for them the teaching of the law and the exhortation of the prophets were a living image of God, just as Paul asserts that in his preaching the glory of God shines in the face of Christ [2 Cor. 4:6]....

Sometimes by the term "church" it means that which is actually in God's presence, into which no persons are received but those who are children of God by grace of adoption and true members of Christ by sanctification of the Holy Spirit.... Often, however, the name "church" designates the whole multitude of people spread over the earth who profess to worship one God and Christ. By baptism we are initiated into faith in Him; by partaking in the Lord's Supper we attest our unity in true doctrine and love; in the word of the Lord we have agreement, and for the preaching of the word the ministry instituted by Christ is preserved. In this church are mingled many hypocrites who have nothing of Christ but the name and outward appearance. There are very many ambitious, greedy, envious persons, evil speakers, and some of quite unclean life. Such are tolerated for a time either because they cannot be convicted by a competent tribunal or because a vigorous discipline does not always flourish as it ought.

Just as we must believe, therefore, that the former church, invisible to us, is visible to the eyes of God alone, so we are commanded to revere and keep communion with the latter [visible one], which is called "church" in respect to earthly observers.

Accordingly, the Lord by certain marks and tokens has pointed out to us what we should know about the church. As we have cited above from Paul [2 Tim. 2:19], to know who are His is a prerogative belonging solely to God.... But on the other hand, because He foresaw it to be of some value for us to know who were to be counted as His children, He has in this regard accommodated Himself to our capacity. And, since assurance of faith was not necessary, He substituted for it a certain charitable judgment whereby we recognize as members of the church those who by profession of faith, by example of life, and by partaking of the sacraments profess the same God and Christ with us. He has, moreover, set off by plainer marks the knowledge of His very body to us, knowing how necessary it is to our salvation.

From this the face of the church comes forth and becomes visible to our eyes. Wherever we see the word of God purely preached and heard and the sacraments administered according to Christ's institution, there, it is not to be doubted, a church of God exists....

Not only does the Lord through forgiveness of sins receive and adopt us once for all into the church, but through the same means He preserves and protects us there.... Consequently, we must firmly believe that by God's generosity, mediated by Christ's merit, through the sanctification of the Spirit, sins have been and are daily pardoned to us who have been received and engrafted into the body of the church.

8. A Short Treatise on the Lord's Supper

This little treatise of five brief headings, published in 1541, is one of Calvin's most accessible explanations of the Lord's Supper. Here portions of the first three sections are presented in the translation of J. K. S. Reid.

—E. A. McKee

Reason for the Institution of the Holy Supper

As to the first article: since it pleased our loving God to receive us by baptism into His church, which is His house and which He will maintain and govern, and since He has received us not only to keep us as servants, but as His own children, it remains that, to discharge the office of a loving father, He nourish us and provide all that is necessary to life.... But just as God has set all fullness of life in Jesus, in order to communicate it to us by means of Him, so He has ordained His word as instrument by which Jesus Christ, with all His benefits, is dispensed to us. Yet it always remains true that our souls have no other pasture than Jesus Christ.... We have already seen how Jesus Christ is the only provision by which our souls are nourished. But because it is distributed by the word of the Lord, which He has appointed as instrument to this end, it is also called bread and water. Now what is said of the word fitly belongs also to the sacrament of the Supper, by means of which our Lord leads us to communication with Jesus Christ. For seeing we are so foolish that we cannot receive Him with true confidence of heart when He is presented by simple teaching and preaching, the Father, of His mercy, not at all disdaining to condescend in this matter to our infirmity, has desired to attach to His word a visible sign by which He represents the substance of His promises to confirm and fortify us and to deliver us from all doubt and uncertainty....

For this reason, the Lord instituted for us His Supper, in order to sign and seal in our consciences the promises contained in His gospel concerning our being made partakers of His body and blood and to give us certainty and assurance that in this consists our true spiritual nourishment; so that, having such an earnest, we might entertain a right assurance about salvation. Second, for the purpose of inciting us to recognize His great goodness toward us, so that we praise and magnify it more fully. Third, to exhort us to all sanctity and innocence, seeing that we are members of Jesus Christ, and particularly to unity and brotherly charity, as is specially recommended to us in it. When we have noted well these three reasons, which our Lord imposed in ordaining His Supper for us, we shall be in a position to understand both what benefits accrue to us from it and what is our duty in its right use.

Benefits of the Holy Supper

It is now time to come to the second point, namely, to show how profitable the Supper of our Lord is to us, on condition that we make profitable use of it.... Or to explain the matter more simply, as we in ourselves are lacking in all good and have not a particle of what might help us to salvation, the Supper is attestation that, being made partakers of the death and Passion of Jesus Christ, we have everything that is useful and salutary for us. Therefore we can say that the Lord here displays to us all the treasures of His spiritual grace, seeing that He makes us associates of all the blessings and riches of our Lord Jesus Christ. Let us remember, then, that the Supper is given us as a mirror in which we may contemplate Jesus Christ crucified to deliver us from damnation and risen again to procure righteousness and eternal life for us. It is indeed true that this same grace is offered us by the gospel; yet as in the Supper we have a more ample certainty and fuller enjoyment, it is with good reason that we recognize such a fruit as coming from it....

Now, if it be asked nevertheless whether the bread is the body of Christ and the wine His blood, we should reply that the bread and the wine are visible signs which represent to us the body and the blood; but that the name and title of body and blood is attributed to them, because they are as instruments by which our Lord Jesus Christ distributes them to us.... It is a spiritual mystery which cannot be seen by the eye or comprehended by the human understanding. It is therefore symbolized by visible signs, as our infirmity requires, but in such a way that it is not a bare figure, but joined to its reality and substance. It is therefore with good reason that the bread is called body, since not only does it represent it to us, but also presents it to us.... Thus, as a brief definition of this benefit of the Supper, we may say that Jesus Christ is there offered to us that we may possess Him, and in Him all the fullness of His gifts which we can desire; and that in this we have great assistance in confirming our conscience in the faith which we ought to have in Him.

The second benefit which the Supper yields us is that it urges and incites us the better to recognize the blessings which we have received, and daily receive, from the Lord Jesus Christ, so that we may render Him such offering of praise as is His due....

The third benefit consists in our having a vehement incitement to holy living and, above all, to observe charity and brotherly love among us. For since we are there made members of Jesus Christ, being incorporated into Him and united to Him as to our Head, this is good reason, first, that we be conformed to His purity and innocence, and especially that we have to one another such charity and concord as members of the same body ought to have....

The Right Use of the Sacrament

Let us come to the third chief head which we proposed at the beginning of this treatise, that is, to the right use, which consists in observing the institution of our Lord with reverence. For whoever approaches this holy sacrament with contempt or indifference, not caring much about following where our Lord calls him, perversely misuses it and thus contaminates it....

If we wish, then, to communicate worthily in the sacred supper of our Lord, we must hold in firm and hearty confidence the Lord Jesus Christ as our sole righteousness, life, and salvation, receiving and accepting the promises which are given us by Him as certain and assured; renouncing on the other hand all other confidence, in order that, distrusting ourselves and all other creatures, we may rest fully in Him and content ourselves with His grace alone.... Here, then, is how we should come to Him in true repentance, in the remembrance that our life is to be conformed to the example of Jesus Christ. Although this should be general in all parts of our life, yet it has a special application to charity, which is above all recommended to us in this sacrament; for which reason it is called the bond of charity. For as the bread, which is there sanctified for the common use of us all, is made of many grains so mixed together that one cannot be discerned from the other, so ought we to be united among ourselves in one indissoluble friendship.... We must then not at all presume to approach, if we bear any hatred or rancor against any living person and especially any Christian who may be within the unity of the church....

But because no one will be found on earth who has so advanced in faith and sanctity of life that he does not still have much infirmity in the one as in the other, there might be a danger that some good consciences be troubled by what has been said, if one did not obviate it by moderating the commands which we have imposed concerning both faith and repentance. It is a perilous method of teaching that some adopt, to demand a perfect confidence of heart and a perfect penitence and to exclude all who do not have them. For in so doing, all are excluded without exception.... When we feel within us a strong distaste and hatred of all vices, proceeding from the fear of God, and a desire to live well in order to please our Lord, we are fit to partake of the Supper, notwithstanding the vestiges of infirmity which we carry in our flesh. If indeed we were not weak, subject to mistrust, and imperfect in life, the sacrament would be of no service to us, and it would have been superfluous to institute it.

Since, then, it is a remedy which God has given us to assist our frailty, to fortify our faith, to augment our charity, and to further us in all sanctity of life, so far from this making us abstain, we ought the more to make use of it the more we feel oppressed by the disease. For if we allege as pretext for not coming to the Supper that we are still weak in faith or in integrity of life, it is as if a person were to excuse himself from taking medicine because he is sick. This, then, is how the frailty of the faith which we feel in our heart and the imperfections which persist in our life ought to incite us to come to the Supper: as to a remedy designed to correct them. Only let us not come without faith or repentance. Of these, the former is hidden in the heart, and therefore our conscience must testify concerning us before God. The second manifests itself by works, and therefore must be somehow apparent in our life.

As to the time of using it, there can be no certain rule for all. For there are certain particular impediments which excuse a person for absenting himself. And besides we have no express command constraining Christians to make use of it every day it is offered to them. However, if we have careful regard to the end for which our Lord intended it, we should realize that the use of it ought to be more frequent than many make it. For the more infirmity oppresses us, the more frequently we need to have recourse to that which is able and ought to serve to confirm our faith and further us in purity of life. Therefore, the custom ought to be well established in all churches of celebrating the Supper as frequently as the capacity of the people will allow. And each individual in his own place ought to prepare himself to receive it whenever it is administered in the congregation, unless there be some grave hindrance which compels him to abstain....

The excuses which some allege, on the other hand, are very frivolous. Some say that they feel themselves unworthy and under cover of this abstain from it for a whole year. Others, not content with wondering about their worthiness, pretend that they cannot communicate with persons whom they see coming without good preparation. Some again think it is superfluous to use it often, since, if we have once received Jesus Christ, there is no need to return so often afterward to receive Him.

I ask the first, who make a cover of their unworthiness, how their conscience can allow them to remain more than a year in so poor a state that they dare not invoke God directly? For they will confess that it is audacity to invoke God as our Father if we are not members of Jesus Christ. This we cannot be unless the substance and reality of the Supper be fulfilled in us. Now if we have the reality, we are, a fortiori, capable of receiving the sign. It is evident, then, that he who would exempt himself from receiving the Supper because of unworthiness bars himself from praying to God. For the rest, I have no intention of forcing consciences that are tormented with certain scruples, that they present themselves they know not how; I, rather, advise them to wait till the

Lord delivers them. Similarly, if there is a legitimate cause of hindrance, I do not deny that it is lawful to defer coming. Only I would point out that no one ought to remain content for long to abstain from the Supper because of his unworthiness, seeing that to do so deprives him of the communion of the church in which all our good consists. Rather, let him strive to contend against all the impediments which the devil puts before him, in order not to be excluded from so great a benefit and consequently from all the gifts of which absence would deprive him.

The second class [of those with objections] have some plausibility, for they employ the following argument. If it is not allowed to eat the common bread with those who call themselves brothers but lead a dissolute and wicked life, a fortiori, we ought to abstain from communicating with them in the bread of our Lord, which is sanctified to represent and dispense to us the body of Christ. But the reply is not very difficult. It is not the office of each individual to judge and discriminate in order to admit or reject as seems to him good, seeing that this prerogative belongs generally to the church as a whole, or rather to the pastor with the elders whom he ought to have for assisting him in the government of the church. For Paul does not command us to examine others, but each is to examine himself [1 Cor. 11:28]. It is very true that our duty is to admonish those whom we see to live disorderly and, if they will not listen, to advise the pastor of them in order that he take proceedings on the authority of the church. But the right way of withdrawing from the company of the wicked is not to quit the communion of the church. Moreover, it will most frequently happen that sins are not so notorious as to justify going the length of excommunication. For though the pastor in his heart judges someone unworthy, yet he has not the power of pronouncing him to be so or of interdicting him from the Supper, unless he can prove it by an ecclesiastical judgment. In this case, we have no other remedy than to pray to God that He would deliver His church more and more from all scandals and to await the Last Day, when the chaff will be manifestly separated from the good grain.

The third class [of those with objections] have no semblance of plausibility. For this spiritual bread is not given us in order that on the first occasion we eat our fill of it, but rather that, having had some taste of its sweetness, we may long for it the more and use it when it is offered us. This is what we have expounded above, that while we remain in this mortal life Jesus Christ is never communicated to us in such a way that our souls are wholly satisfied with Him, but He desires to be our continual nourishment.

9. Passion Week

*Although after 1550 Geneva did not observe liturgical feasts
such as Christmas and Ascension on the traditional dates and
had also completely dropped such seasons as Advent and Lent,
the city continued the traditional liturgical occasion associated with the most important feast of the year, Easter. At least
from 1544 onward, the week before Easter each year was set
apart as a time for sermons on the Passion of Christ. Presented
here is the sermon preached on Friday, March 27, 1562; my
translation.*

—E. A. McKee

From the sixth hour there was darkness over all the earth
till the ninth hour. About the ninth hour Jesus cried in a
loud voice, "Eli, Eli, lama sabachthani," that is, "My God,
My God, why have You abandoned Me?" And some of
those who were present there, having heard that, said:
"He is calling Elijah." And immediately one of them ran
and took a sponge and having filled it with vinegar he
put it on a reed and gave Him something to drink. The
others said: "Stop, let's see if Elijah will come to deliver
Him." Then Jesus, crying again in a loud voice, gave up
His spirit. And behold, the veil of the temple was torn
into two, from top to bottom, and the earth trembled
and the rocks broke open. And the tombs opened and
after He was resurrected some bodies of the saints who
had been asleep were raised. And coming out of the
tombs they went into the holy city and appeared to some
people. [Matt. 27:45–53; Calvin read to the end of the
chapter, but preached only through v. 53.]

Yesterday we began to see how God allowed His only Son to be extremely humiliated in order to gather us to the eternal glory from which we had been banished. From that we must learn that from one angle, that is, in our sight, this death was very shameful. But Jesus Christ did not fail to triumph over the devil, sin, and the world. So, when St. Paul says [Col. 2:14] that the charge which stood against our salvation was wiped out, he adds that our Lord Jesus Christ bound it to His death and He triumphed over every power, as if He were there on a royal throne. In truth, though death in itself was cursed in its nature, yet when the Son of God was put to death, the angels worshiped Him there as their chief and sovereign prince. And if we consider the power of His death and the fruit that comes to us from it, we will find it not at all a curse, but it will be the fountain of justice, life, and salvation. This, then, is what we must remember: when it is said that our Lord Jesus Christ was as if destroyed with shame, let us know that it was in our persons, and let us be horrified and confounded by our sins, seeing that our salvation cost Him so dearly. However, let us also know that His shameful death was not endured for His majesty or His divine glory, and even that it did not diminish the honor which belongs to Him as our mediator. On the contrary, since His inestimable goodness shines in His suffering so much for us, that ought to incite us to be caught up to glorify Him more.

In fact, what is told about one of the thieves is a part of this article that I have said. Because, after he has recognized and confessed that our Lord Jesus Christ is righteous and that it is not for

His own misdeeds that He suffers, and after recognizing also his own poverty and condemning himself out of his own mouth, the thief prays and shows a faith as fine as can be found in any living creature. He says: "Lord, remember me, when You come into Your kingdom" [Luke 23:42]. We must note the circumstances of the time: In what situation does he see our Lord Jesus Christ? He sees Him hung there on a gibbet, which was cursed even by the sentence of God and not only by human opinion. For it is written in the law: "Cursed be one who is hung on the wood" [Deut. 21:23]. See, therefore, our Lord Jesus Christ has been cursed. The thief sees Him near to death, being mocked on one side, blasphemed on the other. In short, if this poor man had been brought up from childhood on the law and prophets and had studied them day and night, this temptation would be likely to turn him away and upset all the instruction he had previously received. For we well see that for the least scandal some people are turned away from the gospel and Christianity—indeed, even those who seem to be the most advanced in it. If, therefore, this poor man had had so much teaching as one could wish, it would serve to swallow up all his faith and cast him into despair when he looked at such a spectacle. He was like someone torn away from his mind, without fear or honor, a poor murderer who had tasted scarcely a bit of God and religion.

And he here sees our Lord Jesus Christ in such a scandalous situation, and yet he calls Him king. How is that? Does he see Him in royal majesty? So we see that God gave him a wonderful faith. And that is why I said yesterday that we shall have greatly profited in our whole life when we have been students of this thief, since he teaches that our Lord Jesus Christ can save poor sinners and he applies this to himself. For since he had continued for a long time in murders and every cruelty and rebellion and was guilty of all kinds of crimes, it is amazing that he could taste the mercy of God and then seek it in our Lord Jesus Christ—seeing Him in such a state. Yet nevertheless he affirms that our Lord Jesus Christ will have mercy on him, and behold he is content and satisfied, as if he had received the fulfillment of complete happiness and joy. However, he was not without feeling. Even his arms and legs were broken, and he had already suffered a great deal of torment. So in the midst of his sufferings, when he had no other concern except to obtain mercy for his sins, and that by means of our Lord Jesus Christ, nevertheless he sees Him crucified there next to him as his companion. In that (as I have said) we must well remember a good teaching from such an example: not only to value what is told us here in order to magnify the virtue of this poor man, but so that we may exercise a true constancy when we are surrounded by many temptations—so that, when heaven and earth have conspired against us to cast us into the deepest depths, we may not on that account cease to take courage and address ourselves to our Lord Jesus Christ.

It is said that the sun gave witness to its Creator at the same time, because its light failed from the sixth hour to the ninth. We must note here that in that time the hours were counted differently from today. They began the hours at the dawn of day, and as the days lengthened so did the hours, for there were never but twelve hours; and as the night lengthened, the hours also lengthened in proportion as they did in the day. Therefore, when it speaks of the sixth hour, it was right at noon that the sun was darkened till the ninth hour, which was the third hour before the night. Thus it was six hours before night when the sun began to lose its light. And so we see that this darkening and eclipse was a certain and notable sign that our Lord Jesus Christ was the Son of the living God. We must not think that the darkness was seen throughout the world; also it could not serve as a sign except to this nation and to the country of Judea.

There was also at the end an upheaval of nature, as if there were good reason to be frightened when our Lord Jesus Christ thus put out the light of the sun. Some think that this was a figure for the blindness that had come upon that Jewish people, others that it was necessary that all righteousness be extinguished and that there must be only dissipation among that people. But it ought to be enough for us that our Lord Jesus Christ wanted to show an uncommon power, so that everyone might be attentive and not cease to glorify Him in His death, however that was mixed up with humiliation, as we have seen.

Be that as it may, behold, the sun is a witness to the divine majesty of our Lord Jesus Christ, there where our natural reason would find it strange. As when Moses also calls the heaven and earth to witness [Deut. 4:26] and the prophet Isaiah says: "Hear, earth, and you, heavens, give ear" [1:2]. Though these are not sentient creatures, yet we see that even though there is no intelligence there, God does not cease to act when He pleases. For the sun and the earth must indeed be teachers of the Jews, and if they had been able to receive this warning that was given to them, it would have converted them and been the means to draw them to salvation. How much more worthy of condemnation, then, is their hardness and diabolic stubbornness when they were not moved, even though the nature of all the elements changed! The earth shook, there where God had given it stability so that we could live on it; the sun lost its light, which by its proper nature lights up all the world. When, then, God spoke by such power and the Jews continued to be unheeding, we see that they were like animals. And that is an example for us that ought to lead us to fear God when we see that those who are rebuked do not change at all, even though God makes such creatures as the sun and earth change. When it speaks of deaf and dumb creatures and that God imprints His power on these visible things and yet they [the Jews] remain blind—when we see that, let us learn to pray that He may make us profit from contemplating His works and that we may devote our study to that, as it is our true wisdom.

It is said that at the ninth hour our Lord Jesus Christ cried: "Eli, Eli, lama sabachthani" [Matt. 27:46]. But this word is a little corrupted. When one changes from one language to another, one always changes some syllables. But be that as it may, it was not without cause that the Evangelist wanted to recite the exact words of our Lord Jesus Christ, in order to alert us that here is one of the principal articles of our faith in this cry of our Lord Jesus Christ. It is taken from Psalm 22 [v. 1], where David (as we have recounted previously) figuratively represents the mediator; there he does not speak in his own name and does not so much put forth his private cause as he tells what had to be accomplished in the One who had been promised as savior.

There He is in extremity and He begins with these words: "My God, My God, why have You abandoned Me?" In this we see how our Lord Jesus Christ not only suffered in His body, but also in His soul. In fact, it would be a great absurdity to say that He was the savior only of our bodies. To bring about our salvation He had to pay the debt of our sins, and the corruption of our offenses was upon Him in order to reconcile us to God, as Isaiah says [53:5]. We know that our bodies are not culpable in themselves; they are muddied with the sins we commit, but still the root of all sin is in the soul. So it was necessary for our Lord Jesus Christ to bear a spiritual punishment in order to gain acquittal and absolution for us from God; that is why He was cast into such anguish in addition to the suffering of death. If you said that this phrase is not suitable for the person of the Son of God, because it is words of despair that God had abandoned Him, the answer is easy. There is no great difficulty in refuting the audacity and malice of His detractors, who want to cut away the most important part of our salvation when they say that our Lord Jesus Christ did not speak according to His own feelings and never felt any fear of the judgment of God, since He was there in the person of evildoers.

For there is a great difference between the natural feelings and emotions that we have and faith. Why? According to our feelings we do not see the life that is prepared for us. It is hidden, says St. Paul [Col. 3:3]; otherwise there would be no place for hope. Yet we

see life, since faith is a sight of things that cannot be seen to appear
[Heb. 11:1]. Thus, according to our natural feelings we only see
death all around; as St. Paul says in the other passage: "We are dead,
our life is hidden in God and in our Lord Jesus Christ." It is as if the
Apostle said: "We are earth and ashes; we feel a fear of death." As
in truth we must always return to this point to humble ourselves,
inasmuch as it is part of every affliction. Our natural feelings, I say,
side with what they apprehend, in accordance with our experience
that God sends us afflictions. That arouses bitterness; we are angry
and sad. However, faith battles against all our human emotions.
And so it happens that though we are still sad, we do not cease to
taste the goodness of God; when we are terrified, we do not cease
to hope in God; and when we are like those who are very agitated
and so lost, we do not cease to flee to Him, having our refuge in
God, who calls us and brings us to Himself. See why St. Paul says in
the Second Epistle to the Corinthians that when we are oppressed,
we are not completely crushed, and if we are dead, we will not
remain there in a pit of hell but will be drawn back [4:9]. In fact,
that is clear enough in these words of our Lord Jesus Christ. For
here there are two parts, which are contraries, but they fit together
very well when we understand how to distinguish between faith
and natural human feelings.

Here it says: "My God, My God." It is certain that we ought to
use these words without hypocrisy (I say), that is, not unless we
are convinced and persuaded that God is our Father and that He
acknowledges us as His children. For we must always come back
to this point: "I shall call you My people and you will call Me

your God" [Lev. 26:12]. If we do not have a sure witness that we are His people, our mouths will be closed and we will be unable to hope that He will be propitious to us. When, then, our Lord Jesus Christ uses that title, let us not petition Him lightly, but let us call upon Him truthfully, with certitude of faith that He is watching over our salvation. And our Lord Jesus Christ was not satisfied to have said "My God" once, but He repeats it. And though that might be in order to fight against the temptation of the flesh, still He affirms at the same time that without doubt He recognizes that God is favorable to Him and is His savior. See, then, the kind of integrity of faith we should desire.

However, He adds, "You have abandoned Me," according to human feeling, but that does not prevent Him from always hoping in God. And see why it is also said that we must hope beyond all hope [Rom. 4:18]; that is, that even though the occasion does not present itself for us to entrust ourselves to God, still we must imitate our Lord Jesus Christ and have all our natural feelings overcome and beaten down and held captive, so that faith may rule over all. See, then, what we are shown in this cry of our Lord Jesus Christ. Now, it was necessary that He come to that point, so that we might be assured that we will never be abandoned by God, whatever may happen, as if He had withdrawn from us and rejected us. Knowing that our Chief fought against such temptations, we must be reformed to be like Him.

Let us never lose courage or cease to pray to God when it appears that He is opposed to us and even armed to thunder against us; let us not cease to return to Him and to call Him our

God, whatever may happen. See, then, how in the midst of our anguish, when it appears that we must be brought down to the depths of hell, we ought nevertheless to strengthen ourselves and renounce all our human emotions, so that God may be glorified. And so we may show that the faith we have in Him is not founded on what can be seen today, but that it rises above all struggles and grasps things invisible. And though we may not at all grasp that God wants to save us, let us nevertheless wait in patience for His help, inasmuch as He has promised it. Let us not measure His power according to our perceptions and what can be seen with the eye, but [rather let us measure it] by this image that is offered us here in His promise by which He opens the heavens for us. So that, if we are afflicted in this life, nevertheless we do not cease to have what we seek in our Lord Jesus Christ, when we are patient and we do Him the honor of hoping for what we do not today see, as we have said. And that is it for this point, where our Lord Jesus Christ laments that He is abandoned by God His Father.

Look how the scribes and priests still mock Him. Because there is no intention of attributing to the soldiers the mockery described here, where our Lord Jesus Christ calls: "Eli, Eli, lama hazabathani." So then there is no doubt that it was in mockery that they [the scribes and priests] changed that word there, which means "My God," into "lama sabachthani." And in fact the Jews could not have had any doubt or ambiguity about those words. In short, they mocked with a certain malice in corrupting the cry of our Lord Jesus Christ, such that when He called on God, they refer it to Elijah, as if He were a profane man and were calling on the dead as the pagans do. In short, it is as if He had no salvation in Himself, and, seeing that He got no more help from God and received no care from Him, He had departed from God and awaited help from Elijah. And so they said: "Let's see if Elijah will come to help Him" [Matt. 27:49]. Behold a rage still more monstrous! That these miserable people, ones who despise God, here mock the name of God and make it a laughing matter and calumny. What an intolerable blasphemy! But they had to show on their side that the devil completely possessed them. And yet our Lord Jesus Christ was subjected to such temptations, so that today we may not find anything strange when we must pass that way. And in accordance with how He shows us the path, let us not doubt that He will lead us to the right way and place of honor. As for the rest, let us know that God watches over us; that today, even in the midst of our struggles, we can triumph fearlessly, knowing that the victory acquired for us by the Son of God belongs to us; and that it was for our profit and not for Himself that He thus powerfully fought and overcame all assaults directed against Him.

Then it is also added that "the veil of the temple was torn" [Matt. 27:51]. That was to break open their hearts, unless they were hardened to the last degree, because they ought to know why this veil had been put in the temple. It divided their sanctuary in such a way as to hinder the people from entering into the presence of God, because the only one who could enter was the priest who brought the incense and offered the solemn sacrifice—the people were excluded. It is true that the priests bore the names of the tribes of Israel in order to give access to God to all, but still the people were kept at a distance. Nevertheless, this was not to prevent entrance to the sanctuary, but to keep them humble, because the glory of God and His abiding place should not be open to their acquaintance. However, they ought to know well that all these figures were only for a time, so that they might always be maintained in anticipation of the mediator who was promised to them. They could well understand that the joy for which we should hope is to rejoice in God's presence, but the veil was interposed. So then by this they were warned that God would never come close to His own until the coming of the Redeemer. Therefore, when today they see the veil of the temple torn, it is as though He revealed Himself in His Son, as if to say: "Here I am, receive Me as your King and Savior!"

But however that ought to profit them, still they are even more hardened, because there was another veil that blinded them and covered their face, as St. Paul says [2 Cor. 3:7–16], citing what is told of the former people: that they could not bear the rays from the face of Moses so he had to wear a cloth [over his face (Exod. 34:29–35)]. St. Paul says what that veil was: it was of dark shadows, and that then there was no illumination such as we have today in the gospel. Because God has appeared in the person of His Son, so that we might not be held in figures with them. But St. Paul speaks of another veil, that is, the stubbornness of the Jews, who are completely blind, because even though they have the law of Moses and they are practiced in it, still they do not see a bit. For what is the law without

Jesus Christ? It is a body without a soul. And when the Jews do not look to Him and they are excluded and alienated, behold their veil: they are completely blind, such that they cannot draw near to Him. When, then, the veil of the temple was torn, that did them no good. But let us apply all this to our instruction. When we see that this veil has been torn, let us know that the ceremonies of the law are ended, and now we have the truth and substance of everything in our Lord Jesus Christ; as St. Paul says, this is the body, while the patriarchs had only the shadow [Col. 2:17]. Then let us know that all the ceremonies which there were under the law have been broken and abolished by the coming of the Son of God, because in Him we have the perfection of what was then in figures.

For the rest, let us recognize the inestimable benefit God has given us: that we do enter not into a temporal and material sanctuary to draw near Him, but by faith and prayers and speech we can easily come to God with our heads up, because the law is fulfilled in us by the blood of our Lord Jesus Christ. Seeing, then, that there is now no veil as there was in the time of the law, let us recognize the privilege that God has given us, that we may call upon Him freely. For our Lord Jesus Christ did not enter there [the sanctuary] for Himself, but for us and in our name. By His means we have such access to God His Father that there is no doubt that He will receive our prayers as if we were spotless, even though we are only corruption and earthworms, sticking to the earth. See what we must remember.

In order to be more confirmed in this teaching, let us add

what is recounted by St. John, where our Lord Jesus Christ says that "all is accomplished" [John 19:30]. For it is in virtue of this word that the veil was torn, because if anything had been lacking of what was figured under the law, it is certain that that would have continued always. But when perfection has come, what was ordained to lead the people to anticipate the Redeemer would be useless and superfluous today. And not only that, but it would be an injury to us, since each would create his own helps according to his fancy. As the papists have turned everything upside down by their follies, devoting themselves to fables and what they have made up, the imitation of the saints, which does nothing except to turn us away from the coming of our Lord Jesus Christ and envelop us such that there is nothing but confusion.

Let us note well, then, and weigh this word where it is said that "all is accomplished," because by that our Lord Jesus Christ wishes to set underfoot all that had then been practiced. And when the sacrifices of the law are spoken about, we know that they pointed to this perfection of our Lord Jesus Christ, which is now accomplished. When, then, we have one perfect One, let us not do as the papists do, who want to have a thousand and an infinite number each day, as they say that this stinking Mass is a sacrifice for the living and the dead. On the contrary, since our Lord Jesus Christ has spoken this definitive sentence, "All is accomplished," it would only be blasphemy and abomination before God if we wanted to have other sacrifices than that which was accomplished in the death of the Son of God. See, then, how this tearing of the veil was an authentic signature of this word of our Lord Jesus Christ, so that we might seek the perfection of all that is required for our salvation in what He has done and suffered.

Then it is said that "the tombs were opened and after the resurrection of our Lord Jesus Christ some of the saints were seen in the holy city" [Matt. 27:52–53]. In this we have confirmation of what I mentioned before, that in things both high and low God wished to give proof for His only Son, so that His death was shown everywhere. But it is particularly said of the tombs so that this word would be manifest. And so they would also know that our Lord Jesus Christ was not resurrected for Himself or His own profit, but He was the firstborn from among the sleeping dead, as St. Paul says in First Corinthians 15 [15:20ff.]. This does not contradict the common teaching where it is said that our life is hidden and the time of our resurrection has not come until our Lord Jesus Christ will come again. Because these two things can go together quite well, that is, that God wished to show these dead among the living for a time so that it might be certified that our Lord Jesus Christ was not resurrected for Himself, but for the whole body of His church.

However, that does not detract from the glory He had even if He had to be [...], as when Enoch and Elijah were taken up into heaven [Gen. 5:24; 2 Kings 2:11]. (It is not that they were glorified in all glory, as that is promised to all the children of God, but God took them as though in trust and reserved for that day.) Thus those here could have been held in reserve after they were seen in Jerusalem; God took them into His keeping, and they will share in the same glory with us, and they await us there. See, then, how there is no contradiction. There was a special resurrection, which was earthly—that is, what happened was not to renew completely those resurrected ones. But it was to give them such life that people might recognize that our Lord Jesus Christ should draw after Him out of death into life those who had been given to Him by God His Father. To argue about how they live and in what state they are now is not appropriate; it would be better to go on soberly, because we ought always to keep to the purity and righteousness of God. Then we have said why they were raised, which is so that the teaching of St. Paul in the Second Epistle to the Corinthians [chap. 5] might be confirmed to us: since our Lord Jesus Christ is raised, let us not doubt our resurrection, because we are as if united inseparably to Him. So much, then, for this point.

That the city of Jerusalem is called "holy city" is not to honor the inhabitants, because they were then worse than Sodom and Gomorrah. It is called "holy" by Isaiah [48:2], and then it came to such an extremity that the people renounced Him who had adopted them as His people—that is indeed to render them more abominable before Him. But we also see that the grace of God can never be wiped out by human malice, as St. Paul shows us that He will be magnified in the midst of perverse people, the wicked and the dissolute [Rom. 3:3; 11:28–29]. And if there were not ministers or prophets or teachers, still the Holy Spirit will always witness to His glory and majesty, and His promises will always be in force, as we also see that our Lord Jesus Christ witnesses to Himself when He says: "Come to Me and you will have abundance of life" [John 10:10; Matt. 11:28–30]. But that is not to say that all those who come there to Him will profit, because to all hypocrites it will serve as a curse to have so profaned such a good thing. But also such profane people cannot destroy this promise, which belongs to all true believers. So then, nevertheless, the holiness our Lord put in Jerusalem was to double the condemnation of the people, that instead of this place being an earthly paradise as it ought, it was only a stinking thing and contagion. This is said so we may learn always to magnify God in all His graces, and at the same time let us also seek to use them worthily and fear to abuse them, lest they come back as a worse curse on us. So much for this point.

It is said that our Lord Jesus Christ "crying again in a loud voice, gave up His spirit" [Matt. 27:50]. St. Luke tells what this cry was and what its content was, that is, He said: "I commend to You My soul, Lord" [Luke 23:46]. See, then, the second cry of the Son of God, which is very different from the first. Because there is first this cry that He is abandoned. And now He commends His soul into the hands of God His Father and gives it to Him, knowing that He will be a good and faithful guardian. Thus we see that in His first lament our Lord Jesus Christ struggled so well that the witness had already come, that He could peacefully say: "My God, I commend to You My soul, and it will be safe when You take it in Your charge and it is in Your protection." We see, then, how it has been shown previously that our Lord Jesus Christ, in making His cries, directed them to the end where we must follow after Him also. That is, that we not feed on what can draw us to defy God, but we must set all that underfoot so as to resist all temptations and call on God freely, as is now done by His Son our Lord Jesus Christ.

Now this is taken from Psalm 31, where we see that, in the midst of danger, David commended his soul into the hands of God [31:5], and this was to signify that God could well save him, were he attacked by a hundred thousand deaths. David does not speak of commending his soul into His hands as if he meant to depart from this world, but it was in order that He might preserve David's soul until the time of his death. It is certain that David could not speak so, did he not pass through death and rise above the blows of this world, because this dwelling place ought not so to hold us that we do not have our regard lifted higher. As it is said in the psalm, we must seek to be so peaceable on earth in order to have lasting peace there above in heaven. David, then, would have had a very slight hope if he had rested his confidence here below. So there is no doubt but that he committed himself into God's hands for life and for death.

Now our Lord Jesus Christ gives the second cry, that is, He commits His soul into the hands of God His Father, even though it appears that it must die. Because while we are sojourning on the earth, still we can hope in some way that God will have us in His keeping and we will be protected by His power. But in death all will fail, if we take the counsel of human feelings, and one cannot think that a person is different from a donkey or a dog, as Solomon says: his nature is like that of the beasts. So we must come to this stance, which is that God may receive our souls in trust and He may be their guardian to keep them in peace. And let us not doubt that in dying we will live forever, inasmuch as if we die in this world and to visible sight, God will not cease to be our Father, and thus our life will rest in His mercy, it will endure always. See in sum what we must remember.

Let us note that our Lord Jesus Christ did not speak thus for Himself. It is true that when He cried out in a loud voice, the zeal and ardor in Him incited Him to do so; nevertheless, He made this petition public in order to put in our mouths the same words, and for us to call upon God at the point of death and for us to commit ourselves into His hands. When (I say) our Lord Jesus Christ formed this petition, it was not for Himself alone, but it is common to all the faithful. This voice ought always to resound in our ears, and we should so listen to the Son of God that the sufferings which assail us may not turn us away from Him who is the Author of our salvation, so that we may remit our souls into His hand and never doubt that we will be heard.

And our Lord Jesus Christ has not only given us such an example, but at the same time He acquired the privilege of being the guardian of our souls, as St. Stephen shows. Because just as our Lord Jesus Christ called upon God His Father, also St. Stephen called upon Him at his death: "Jesus Christ," he says, "I commend my soul into Your hands" [Acts 7:59]. He does not speak at random. For what does it mean to commend our souls into the hand of a protector? There must be all-divine power. Now, St. Stephen recognized that our Lord Jesus Christ was consecrated to God His

Father, the protector of our souls—that is for our instruction, so that we may always be bold to commend ourselves to Him. As He exhorts us in the tenth chapter of St. John, when He says that we are in His care and that all who have been committed to Him will have such a good guardian that none will be lost till the last day, when He will give accounting to God His Father [10:28].

See, then, what we also must remember, that in dying we may not think that we are only emptying a breath into the air, but let us know that the souls which God created will return into His hand and will be kept until all will be restored in glory eternal. It is said that our Lord Jesus Christ died, so that we may know that He was the firstborn of the dead. Because if He had only come up to the point of death and God had delivered Him from it, what would that be to us when we are dying? We would be like people gone astray and lost. But when our Lord Jesus Christ goes before us even when we are dying, in that lies our hope—see how we can persevere in calling upon Him! Let us note well, then, that our Lord Jesus Christ not only died after He had been condemned under Pontius Pilate, but He was raised so that we might be completely and throughout united and joined with Him; and that we might willingly follow Him to death with a true hope that we will share in His death and in His resurrection, to experience their fruit, because by that [death and resurrection] the devil is overcome.

We bow ourselves before the majesty of our good God in recognition of so many faults of which we are guilty, praying that He may be pleased to make us so much profit from what we have now heard that we may be more and more attentive to a true repentance, to condemn in ourselves our vices. And that we may also have our refuge in our Lord Jesus Christ, to cast ourselves completely on Him and there have our whole refuge and resting place; and never to doubt that, when God is pleased to receive us into His keeping, though there may be only misery in all our life, and death may be horrifying to our natural feeling and judgment, still we will never fail to have lasting life and to be companions of the angels when we are brought under His hands. And may He grant this not only to us, but to all peoples and nations on earth....

III. THE CHRISTIAN LIFE

10. Exposition of the Lord's Prayer

The fundamental Christian prayer is the Lord's Prayer, and Calvin, like most teachers before and after him, made the exposition of this prayer central to his instruction as well as to his liturgical practice. Here is presented an abbreviated form of his teaching in the Institutes, Book Three, Chapter 20. The translation is by F. L. Battles. Since Calvin's name is usually associated primarily with the doctrine of predestination, it is worth noting that in explaining the Lord's Prayer the theologian-pastor insists that the Christian prays "not only for those whom he at present sees and recognizes as [his brothers in Christ], but [for] all people who dwell on earth."

—E. A. McKee

First, at the very threshold we meet what I previously mentioned: we ought to offer all prayer to God only in Christ's name, as it cannot be agreeable to Him in any other name. For in calling God "Father," we put forward the name "Christ." With what confidence would anyone address God as "Father"? Who would break forth into such rashness as to claim for himself the honor of a son of God unless we had been adopted as children of grace in Christ? He, although He is the true Son, has of Himself been given us as a brother that what He has of His own by nature may become ours by benefit of adoption if we embrace this great blessing with sure faith.... Thus, if we are His sons, we cannot seek help anywhere else than from Him without reproaching Him with cruelty and excessive rigor.

And let us not pretend that we are justly rendered timid by the consciousness of sins, since sins daily make our Father, although kind and gentle, displeased with us…. He depicts and represents for us in a parable this abundance of fatherly compassion: a son had estranged himself from his father, had dissolutely wasted his substance, had grievously offended him in every way; but the father embraces him with open arms, and does not wait for him to ask for pardon but anticipates him, recognizes him returning afar off, willingly runs to meet him, comforts him, receives him into favor [Luke 15:20]. For in setting forth this example of great compassion to be seen in a person, He willed to teach us how much more abundantly we ought to expect it of Him…. But because the narrowness of our hearts cannot comprehend God's boundless favor, not only is Christ the pledge and guarantee of our adoption, but He gives the Spirit as witness to us of the same adoption, through whom with free and full voice we may cry, "Abba, Father." Therefore, whenever any hesitation shall hinder us, let us remember to ask Him to correct our fearfulness and to set before us that Spirit that He may guide us to pray boldly.

However, we are not so instructed that each one of us should individually call Him his Father, but rather that all of us in common should call Him our Father. From this fact we are warned how great a feeling of brotherly love ought to be among us, since by the same right of mercy and free liberality we are equally children of such a father [Matt. 23:9]. For if one father is common to us all and every good thing that can fall to our lot comes from Him, there ought not to be anything separate among us that we are not prepared gladly and wholeheartedly to share with one another, as far as occasion requires.

Now if we so desire, as is fitting, to extend our hand to one another and to help one another, there is nothing in which we can benefit our brethren more than in commending them to the providential care of the best of fathers; for if He is kind and favorable, nothing at all else can be desired. Indeed, we owe even this very thing to our Father. Just as one who truly and deeply loves any father of a family at the same time embraces his whole household with love and goodwill, so it becomes us in like measure to show to His people, to His family, and, last, to His inheritance the same zeal and affection that we have toward this heavenly Father. For He so honored these as to call them the fullness of His only begotten Son [Eph. 1:23]. Let the Christian, then, conform his prayers to this rule in order that they may be in common and embrace all who are his brothers in Christ, not only those whom he at present sees and recognizes as such, but all people who dwell on earth. For what God has determined concerning them is beyond our knowing except that it is no less devout than humane to wish and hope the best for them. Yet we ought to be drawn with a special affection to those, above others, of the household of faith, whom the Apostle has particularly commended to us in everything [Gal. 6:10]. To sum up, all prayers ought to be such as to look to that community our Lord has established in His kingdom and His household.

Nevertheless, this does not prevent us from praying especially for ourselves and for certain others, provided, however, that our minds do not withdraw their attention from this community or turn aside from it but refer all things to it. For although prayers are individually framed, since they are directed to this end, they do not cease to be common. All this can easily be understood by a comparison. There is a general command of God's to relieve the need of all the poor, and yet those obey it who to this end succor the indigence of those whom they know or see to be suffering, even though they overlook many who are pressed by no lighter need because either they cannot know all or cannot provide for all. In this way they who, viewing and pondering this common society of the church, frame particular prayers of this sort do not resist the will of God when in their prayers, with God's people at heart, in particular terms they commend to God themselves or others whose needs He has been pleased to make intimately known to them.

However, not all aspects of prayer and almsgiving are indeed alike. For liberality of giving can be practiced only toward those whose poverty is visible to us. But we are free to help by prayer even utterly foreign and unknown persons, however great the distance that separates them from us. This too is done through that general form of prayer wherein all children of God are included, among whom they also are. To this may be referred the fact that Paul urges the believers of his time to lift pure hands in every place without quarreling [1 Tim. 2:8]. In warning them that strife shuts the gate to prayers, his intention is that they offer their petitions in common with one accord.

That He is in heaven is added.... By this He obviously means that He is not confined to any particular region, but is diffused through all things.... But while we hear this, our thought must be raised higher when God is spoken of, lest we dream up anything earthly or physical about Him, lest we measure Him by our small measure or conform His will to our emotions. At the same time our confidence in Him must be aroused, since we understand that heaven and earth are ruled by His providence and power.

To sum up: under the name "Father" is set before us that God who appeared to us in His own image that we should call upon Him with assured faith. And not only does the intimate name "Father" engender trust, but it is effective also to keep our minds from being drawn away to doubtful and false gods, permitting them to rise up from the only begotten Son to the sole Father of angels and of the church. Second, because His throne is established in heaven, from His governing of the universe we are forcibly reminded that we do not come to Him in vain, for He willingly meets us with present help.... Here Christ declares both of these things to His Father: that our faith rests in Himself, then that we should surely be persuaded that our salvation is not overlooked by Him. For He deigns to extend His providence even to us....

The first petition is that God's name be hallowed; the need for it is associated with our great shame. For what is more unworthy than for God's glory to be obscured partly by our ungratefulness, partly by our ill will, and, so far as lies in our power, destroyed by our presumption and insane impudence? Though all the ungodly should break out with their sacrilegious license, the holiness of

God's name still shines.... Because, therefore, God's holiness is so unworthily snatched from Him on earth, if it is not in our power to assert it, at least we are bidden to be concerned for it in our prayers.

To summarize: we should wish God to have the honor He deserves; people should never speak or think of Him without the highest reverence.... Here we are bidden to request not only that God vindicate His sacred name of all contempt and dishonor, but also that He subdue the whole human race to reverence for it. Now since God reveals Himself to us partly in teaching, partly in works, we can hallow Him only if we render to Him what is His in both respects, and so embrace all that proceeds from Him. And His sternness no less than His leniency should lead us to praise Him, seeing that He has engraved marks of His glory upon a manifold diversity of works, and this rightly calls forth praises from every tongue. Thus it will come about that Scripture will obtain a just authority among us, nor will anything happen to hinder us from blessing God, as in the whole course of His governance of the universe He deserves....

The second petition is that God's kingdom come. Even though it contains nothing new, it is with good reason kept separate from the first petition; for if we consider our languor in the greatest matters of all, it behooves us to extend our discussion in order to drive home something that ought to have been thoroughly known of itself.... God reigns where people, both by denial of themselves and by contempt of the world and of earthly life, pledge themselves to His righteousness in order to aspire to a heavenly life. Thus there are two parts to this kingdom: first, that God by the power of His Spirit correct all the lusts of the flesh which by squadrons war against Him; second, that He shape all our thoughts in obedience to His rule. Therefore, no others keep a lawful order in this petition but those who begin with themselves, that is, to be cleansed of all corruptions that disturb the peaceful state of God's kingdom and sully its purity. Now, because the word of God is like a royal scepter, we are bidden here to entreat Him to bring all people's minds and hearts into voluntary obedience to it. This happens when He manifests the working of His word through the secret inspiration of His Spirit in order that it may stand forth in the degree of honor that it deserves. Afterward we should descend to the impious, who stubbornly and with desperate madness resist His authority.... We must daily desire that God gather churches unto Himself from all parts of the earth; that He spread and increase them in number; that He adorn them with gifts; that He establish a lawful order among them; on the other hand, that He cast down all enemies of pure teaching and religion; that He scatter their counsels and crush their efforts....

Thus this prayer ought to draw us back from worldly corruptions which so separate us from God that His kingdom does not thrive within us. At the same time it ought to kindle zeal for mortification of the flesh; finally, it ought to instruct us in bearing the cross. For it is in this way that God wills to spread His kingdom.... For this is the condition of God's kingdom: that while we submit to His righteousness, He makes us sharers in

His glory.... Meanwhile, He protects His own, guides them by the help of His Spirit into uprightness, and strengthens them to perseverance. But He overthrows the wicked conspiracies of enemies, unravels their stratagems and deceits, opposes their malice, and represses their obstinacy until at last He slays Antichrist with the Spirit of His mouth and destroys all impiety by the brightness of His coming [2 Thess. 2:8].

The third petition is that God's will may be done on earth as in heaven. Even though it depends upon His kingdom and cannot be separated from it, still it is with reason added separately on account of our ignorance, which does not easily or immediately comprehend what it means that "God reigns in the world." It will therefore not be absurd to take it as an explanation that God will be King in the world when all submit to His will. Here it is not a question of His secret will, by which He controls all things and directs them to their end.... But here God's other will is to be noted—namely, that to which voluntary obedience corresponds.... We are therefore bidden to desire that, just as in heaven nothing is done apart from God's good pleasure and the angels dwell together in all peace and uprightness, the earth be in like manner subject to such a rule, with all arrogance and wickedness brought to an end.

And in asking this we renounce the desires of our flesh; for whoever does not resign and submit his feelings to God opposes as much as he can God's will, since only what is corrupt comes forth from us. And again by this prayer we are formed to self-denial so God may rule us according to His decision. And not this alone but also so He may create new minds and hearts in us.... In sum, so we may wish nothing from ourselves but that His Spirit may govern our hearts; and while the Spirit is inwardly teaching us we may learn to love the things that please Him and to hate those which displease Him. In consequence, our wish is that He may render futile and of no account whatever feelings are incompatible with His will.

Here, then, are the first three sections of the prayer. In making these requests we are to keep God's glory alone before our eyes, while leaving ourselves out of consideration and not looking to any advantage for ourselves; for such advantage, even though it amply accrues from such a prayer, must not be sought by us here. But even though all these things must nonetheless come to pass in their time, without any thought or desire or petition of ours, still we ought to desire and request them. And it is of no slight value for us to do this. Thus, we may testify and profess ourselves servants and children of God, zealously, truly, and deeply committed, to the best of our ability, to the honor that is owed our Lord and Father. Therefore, those who do not, with this desire and zeal to further God's glory, pray that "God's name be hallowed," that "His kingdom come," that "His will be done" should not be reckoned among God's children and servants; and inasmuch as all these things will come to pass even against such people's consent, the result will be their confusion and destruction.

The second part of the prayer follows, in which we descend to our own affairs. We do not indeed bid farewell to God's glory, which as Paul testifies is to be seen even in food and drink, and we ask only what is expedient for us [1 Cor. 10:31]. But we have pointed out that there is this difference: God specifically claims the first three petitions and draws us wholly to Himself to prove our piety in this way. Then He allows us to look after our own interests, yet under this limitation: that we seek nothing for ourselves without the intention that whatever benefits He confers upon us may show forth His glory, for nothing is more fitting than that we live and die to Him.

But by this petition we ask of God all things in general that our bodies have need to use under the elements of this world, not only for food and clothing but also for everything God perceives to be beneficial to us, that we may eat our daily bread in peace. Briefly, by this we give ourselves over to His care and entrust ourselves to His providence, that He may feed, nourish, and preserve us. For our most gracious Father does not disdain to take even our bodies under His safekeeping and guardianship in order to exercise our faith in these small matters, while we expect everything from Him, even to a crumb of bread and a drop of water. For since it has come about in some way or other through our wickedness that we are affected and tormented with greater concern for body than for soul, many who venture to entrust the soul to God are still troubled about the flesh, still worry about what they shall eat, what they shall wear, and, unless they have on hand abundance of wine, grain, and oil, tremble with apprehension. So much more does the shadow of this fleeting life mean to us than that everlasting immortality. Those who, relying upon God, have once and for all cast out that anxiety about the care of the flesh immediately expect from Him greater things, even salvation and eternal life. It is, then, no light exercise of faith for us to hope for those things from God which otherwise cause us such anxiety. And we benefit greatly when we put off this faithlessness, which clings to the very bones of almost all.

What certain writers say in philosophizing about "supersubstantial bread" seems to me to agree very little with Christ's meaning; indeed, if we did not even in this fleeting life accord to God the office of nourisher, this would be an imperfect prayer. The reason they give is too profane: that it is not fitting that children of God, who ought to be spiritual, not only give their attention to earthly cares, but also involve God in these with themselves. As if His blessing and fatherly favor are not shown even in food, or it were written to no purpose that "piety holds promise not only for the life to come but also for the present life" [1 Tim. 4:8]! Now even though forgiveness of sins is far more important than bodily nourishment, Christ placed the inferior thing first that He might bring us gradually to the two remaining petitions, which properly belong to the heavenly life. In this He has taken account of our slowness.

But we are bidden to ask our daily bread that we may be content with the measure that our heavenly Father has deigned to distribute to us and not get gain by unlawful devices. Meanwhile, we must hold that it is made ours by title of gift; for, as is said in Moses, neither effort nor toil nor our hands acquire anything for us by themselves but by God's blessing [Lev. 26:20]....The word "today" ... bridled the uncontrolled desire for fleeting things.... We are bidden to ask only as much as is sufficient for our need from day to day, with this assurance: that as our heavenly Father nourishes us today, He will not fail us tomorrow. Thus, however abundantly goods may flow to us, even when our storehouses are stuffed and our cellars full, we ought always to ask for our daily bread, for we must surely count all possessions nothing except insofar as the Lord, having poured out His blessing, makes it fruitful with continuing increase. Also, what is in our hand is not even ours except insofar as He bestows each little portion upon us hour by hour and allows us to use it.... He shows it is by His power alone that life and strength are sustained, even though He administers it to us by physical means....

Yet those who, not content with daily bread but panting after countless things with unbridled desire, or sated with their abundance, or carefree in their piled-up riches, supplicate God with this prayer are but mocking Him. For the first ones ask Him what they do not wish to receive, indeed what they utterly abominate—namely, mere daily bread—and as much as possible cover up before God their propensity to greed, while true prayer ought to pour out before Him the whole mind itself and whatever lies hidden within. The others ask of Him what they least expect, that is, what they think they have within themselves. In calling the bread "ours," God's generosity, as we have said, stands forth the more, for it makes ours what is by no right owed to us.... What has been obtained by just and harmless toil is so designated, not what is got by frauds or robberies; for all that we acquire through harming another belongs to another. The fact that we ask that it be given us signifies that it is a simple and free gift of God, however it may come to us, even when it would seem to have been obtained from our own skill and diligence and supplied by our own hands. For it is by His blessing alone that our labors truly prosper.

Next follows: "Forgive us our debts." With this and the following petition, Christ briefly embraces all that makes for the heavenly life, as the spiritual covenant that God has made for the salvation of His church rests on these two members alone: "I shall write my laws upon their hearts" and "I shall be merciful toward their iniquity" [Jer. 31:33; 33:8]. Here Christ begins with forgiveness of sins, then presently adds the second grace: that God protect us by the power of His Spirit and sustain us by His aid, so we may stand unvanquished against all temptations. He calls sins "debts" because we owe penalty for them, and we could in no way satisfy it unless we were released by this forgiveness. This pardon comes of His free mercy, by which He Himself generously wipes out these debts, exacting no payment from us, but making satisfaction to Himself by His own mercy in Christ, who once for all gave Himself as a ransom....

Finally, we petition that forgiveness come to us, "as we forgive our debtors": namely, as we spare and pardon all who have in any way injured us, either treating us unjustly in deed or insulting us in word. Not that it is ours to forgive the guilt of transgression or offense, for this belongs to God alone! This, rather, is our forgiveness: willingly to cast from the mind wrath, hatred, and desire for revenge and willingly to banish to oblivion the remembrance of injustice. For this reason, we ought not to seek forgiveness of sins from God unless we ourselves also forgive the offenses against us of all those who do or have done us ill. If we retain feelings of hatred in our hearts, if we plot revenge and ponder any occasion to cause harm, and even if we do not try to get back into our enemies' good graces, by every sort of good office deserve well of them and commend ourselves to them, by this prayer we entreat God not to forgive our sins....

Finally, we must note that this condition—that He "forgive us as we forgive our debtors"—is not added because by the forgiveness we grant to others we deserve His forgiveness, as if this indicated the cause of it. Rather, by this word the Lord intended partly to comfort the weakness of our faith. For He has added this as a sign to assure us He has granted forgiveness of sins to us just as surely as we are aware of having forgiven others, provided our hearts have been emptied and purged of all hatred, envy, and vengeance. Also, it is partly by this mark that the Lord excludes from the number of His children those persons who, being eager for revenge and slow to forgive, practice persistent enmity and foment against others the very indignation that they pray to be averted from themselves. This the Lord does that such people dare not call upon Him as Father....

The sixth petition, as we have said, corresponds to the promise that the law is to be engraved upon our hearts, but because we obey God not without continual warfare and hard and trying struggles, here we seek to be equipped with such armor and defended with such protection that we may be able to win the victory. By this we are instructed that we need not only the grace of the Spirit to soften our hearts within and to bend and direct them to obey God, but also His aid, to render us invincible against both all the stratagems and all the violent assaults of Satan.... And these temptations are either from the right or from the left. From the right are, for example, riches, power, honors, which often dull people's keenness of sight by the glitter and seeming goodness they display and allure with their blandishments, so that, captivated by such tricks and drunk with such sweetness, they forget their God. From the left are, for example, poverty, disgrace, contempt, afflictions, and the like. Thwarted by the hardship and difficulty of these, they become despondent in mind, cast away assurance and hope, and are at last completely estranged from God. We pray God, our Father, not to let us yield to the two sorts of temptations,... that we may not be puffed up in prosperity or yet cast down in adversity.

Nevertheless, we do not here ask that we feel no temptations at all, for we need, rather, to be aroused, pricked, and urged by them, lest, with too much inactivity, we grow sluggish.... But God tries in one way, Satan in another. Satan tempts that he may destroy, condemn, confound, cast down, but God, that by proving His own children He may make trial of their sincerity and establish their strength by exercising it; that He may mortify, purify, and cauterize their flesh, which unless it were forced under this restraint would play the wanton and vaunt itself beyond measure. Besides, Satan attacks those who are unarmed and unprepared

that he may crush them unaware. God, along with the temptation, makes a way of escape, that His own may be able patiently
to bear all that He imposes upon them. It makes very little difference whether we understand by the word "evil" the devil or sin.
Indeed, Satan himself is the enemy who lies in wait for our life
[1 Pet. 5:8].... Now we seek to be freed from his power, as from
the jaws of a mad and raging lion; if the Lord did not snatch us
from the midst of death, we could not help being immediately
torn to pieces by his fangs and claws and swallowed down his
throat. Yet we know that if the Lord is with us and fights for us
while we keep still, "in His might we shall do mightily" [Ps.
60:12]. Let others trust as they will in their own capacities and
powers of free choice, which they seem to themselves to possess.
For us let it be enough that we stand and are strong in God's
power alone.... While we petition, then, to be freed from Satan
and sin, we anticipate that new increases of God's grace will continually be showered upon us, until, completely filled therewith,
we triumph over all evil.

These three petitions, in which we especially commend to God
ourselves and all our possessions, clearly show what we have previously said: that the prayers of Christians ought to be public and
to look to the public edification of the church and the advancement of the believers' fellowship. For each one does not pray that
something be given to him privately, but all of us in common ask
our bread, forgiveness of sins, not to be led into temptation, and
to be freed from evil....

Moreover, there is added the reason why we should be so bold
to ask and so confident of receiving ... that His "is the kingdom,

and the power, and the glory, forever." This is firm and tranquil repose for our faith. For if our prayers were to be commended to God by our worth, who would dare even mutter in His presence? Now, however miserable we may be, though unworthiest of all, however devoid of all commendation, we will yet never lack a reason to pray, never be shorn of assurance, since His kingdom, power, and glory can never be snatched away from our Father. At the end is added "Amen."... By this the saints not only express the end of their prayers, but confess themselves unworthy to obtain it unless God seeks the reason from Himself, and that their confidence of being heard stems solely from God's nature.

11. The Pattern of the Law for Piety

From the Institutes of the Christian Religion, *Book Two,* The Knowledge of God the Redeemer in Christ. *Prayer may be the chief exercise of piety, but it is not the only one. How Christians live their daily lives is a vital and necessary working out of their relationship with God. For Calvin, this earthly life of Christians, which is transformed because it is claimed by God and lived in God's presence, includes both individual and communal aspects. Here excerpts from Calvin's treatment of several commandments illustrate the supportive structure that the third use of the law offers for the spiritual life.*

—E. A. McKee

The Law Was Given Not to Restrain, but to Foster Hope of Salvation in Christ Until His Coming

The third and principal use, which pertains more closely to the proper purpose of the law, finds its place among believers in whose hearts the Spirit of God already lives and reigns. For even though they have the law written and engraved upon their hearts by the finger of God, that is, have been so moved and quickened through the directing of the Spirit that they long to obey God, they still profit by the law in two ways.

Here is the best instrument for them to learn more thoroughly each day the nature of the Lord's will to which they aspire and to confirm them in the understanding of it. It is as if some servant, already prepared with all earnestness of heart to commend himself to his master, must search out and observe his master's ways more carefully in order to conform and accommodate himself to them. And not one of us may escape from this necessity. For no person has heretofore attained to such wisdom as to be unable, from the daily instruction of the law, to make fresh progress toward a purer knowledge of the divine will.

Again, because we need not only teaching but also exhortation, the servant of God will also avail himself of this benefit of the law: by frequent meditations upon it to be aroused to obedience, be strengthened in it, and be drawn back from the slippery path of transgression....

Explanation of the Moral Law: (The Ten Commandments)
Sixth Commandment: "You shall not kill"

The purpose of this commandment is: the Lord has bound the human race together by a certain unity; hence each person ought to concern himself with the safety of all. To sum up, then, all violence, injury, and any harmful thing at all that may injure our neighbor's body are forbidden to us. We are accordingly commanded, if we find anything of use to us in saving our neighbors' lives, faithfully to employ it; if there is anything that makes for their peace, to see to it; if anything harmful, to ward it off; if they are in any danger, to lend a helping hand. If you recall that God is so speaking as Lawgiver, ponder at the same time that by this rule He wills to guide your soul. For it would be ridiculous that He who looks upon the thoughts of the heart and dwells especially upon them should instruct only the body in true righteousness. Therefore this law also forbids murder of the heart and enjoins the inner intent to save a brother's life. The hand indeed gives birth to murder, but the mind, when infected with anger and hatred, conceives it. See whether you can be angry against your brother without burning with desire to hurt him. If you cannot be angry with him, then you cannot hate him, for hatred is nothing but sustained anger. Although you dissimulate and try to escape by vain shifts—where there is either anger or hatred there is the intent to do harm. If you keep trying to evade the issue, the Spirit has already declared that "he who hates a brother in his heart is a murderer" [1 John 3:15]; the Lord Christ has declared that "Whoever is angry with his brother is liable to judgment; whoever says 'Raca' is liable to the council; whoever says 'You fool!' is liable to the hell of fire" [Matt. 5:22].

Scripture notes that this commandment rests upon a twofold basis: each person is both the image of God and our flesh. Now, if we do not wish to violate the image of God, we ought to hold our neighbor sacred. And if we do not wish to renounce all humanity, we ought to cherish his as our own flesh. We shall elsewhere discuss how this exhortation is to be derived from the redemption and grace of Christ. The Lord has willed that we consider those two things which are naturally in each person and might lead us to seek his preservation: to reverence His image imprinted in each person and to embrace our own flesh in him. He who has merely refrained from shedding blood has not therefore avoided the crime of murder. If you perpetrate anything by deed, if you plot anything by attempt, if you wish or plan anything contrary to the safety of a neighbor, you are considered guilty of murder. Again, unless you endeavor to look out for his safety according to your ability and opportunity, you are violating the law with a like heinousness. But if there is so much concern for the safety of his body, from this we may infer how much zeal and effort we owe the safety of the soul, which far excels the body in the Lord's sight.

Eighth Commandment: "You shall not steal"

The purpose of this commandment is: since injustice is an abomination to God, we should render to each person what belongs to him. To sum up: we are forbidden to pant after the possessions of others and consequently are commanded to strive faithfully to help every person to keep his own possessions. We must consider that what each one possesses has not come to him by mere chance, but by the distribution of the supreme Lord of all things. For this reason, we cannot by evil devices deprive anyone of his possessions without fraudulently setting aside God's dispensation. Now there are many kinds of thefts. One consists in violence, when another's goods are stolen by force and unrestrained brigandage. A second kind consists in malicious deceit, when they are carried off through fraud. Another lies in a more concealed craftiness, when a person's goods are snatched from him by seemingly legal means. Still another lies in flatteries, when one is cheated of his goods under the pretense of a gift.

Let us not stop too long to recount the kinds of theft. Let us remember that all those arts whereby we acquire the possessions and money of our neighbors—when such devices depart from sincere affection to a desire to cheat or in some manner to harm—are to be considered as thefts. Although such possessions may be acquired in a court action, yet God does not judge otherwise. For He sees the intricate deceptions with which a crafty person sets out to snare one of simpler mind, until he at last draws him into his nets. He sees the hard and inhuman laws with which the more powerful oppresses and crushes the weaker person. He sees the lures with which the wilier person baits, so to speak, his hooks to catch the unwary. All these things elude human judgment and are not recognized. And such injustice occurs not only in matters of money or in merchandise or land, but in the right of each one; for we defraud our neighbors of their property if we repudiate the duties by which we are obligated to them. If a shiftless steward or overseer devours his master's substance and fails to attend to household business; if he either unjustly spends or wantonly wastes the properties entrusted to him; if the servant mocks his master; if he divulges his secrets; if in any way he betrays his life or goods; if the master, on the other hand, savagely harasses his household—all these are deemed theft in God's sight. For he who does not carry out what he owes to others according to the responsibility of his own calling both withholds and appropriates what is another's.

We will duly obey this commandment, then, if, content with our lot, we are zealous to make only honest and lawful gain; if we do not seek to become wealthy through injustice or attempt to deprive our neighbor of his goods to increase our own; if we do not strive to heap up riches cruelly wrung from the blood of others; if we do not madly scrape together from everywhere, by fair means or foul, whatever will feed our avarice or satisfy our prodigality. On the other hand, let this be our constant aim: faithfully to help all people by our counsel and aid to keep what is theirs, insofar as we can; but if we have to deal with faithless and deceitful people, let us be prepared to give up something of our own rather than to contend with them. And not this alone: but let us share the necessity of those whom we see pressed by the difficulty of affairs, assisting them in their need with our abundance. Finally, let each one see to what extent he is in duty bound to others, and let him pay his debt faithfully.…

Ninth Commandment: "You shall not be a false witness against your neighbor"

The purpose of this commandment is: since God (who is truth) abhors a lie, we must practice truth without deceit toward one another. To sum up, then: let us not malign anyone with slanders or false charges or harm his substance by falsehood, in short, injure him by unbridled evil speaking and impudence. To this prohibition the command is linked that we should faithfully help everyone as much as we can in affirming the truth, in order to protect the integrity of his name and possessions.… Hence this commandment is lawfully observed when our tongue, in declaring the truth, serves both the good repute and the advantage of our neighbors. The equity of this is quite evident. For if a good name is no less precious than all riches, we harm a person more by despoiling him of the integrity of his name than by taking away his possessions. In plundering his substance, however, we sometimes do as much by false testimony as by snatching with our hands.

And yet it is wonderful with what thoughtless unconcern we sin in this respect time and again. Those who do not markedly suffer from this disease are rare indeed. We delight in a certain poisoned sweetness experienced in ferreting out and in disclosing the evils of others. And let us not think it an adequate excuse if in many instances we are not lying. For he who does not allow a brother's name to be sullied by falsehood also wishes it to be kept unblemished as far as truth permits. Indeed, although he may guard it against lying only, he yet implies by this that it is entrusted to his care. That God is concerned about it should be enough to prompt us to keep safe our neighbor's good name. Hence, evil speaking is without a doubt universally condemned. Now, we understand by "evil speaking" not reproof made with intent to chastise, not accusation or judicial denunciation to remedy evil. Nor does evil speaking mean public correction, calculated to strike other sinners with terror, nor disclosure before those who need to be forewarned lest they be endangered through ignorance. By "evil speaking" we mean hateful accusation arising from evil intent and wanton desire to defame.

Indeed, this precept even extends to forbidding us to affect a fawning politeness barbed with bitter taunts under the guise of joking. Some do this who crave praise for their witticisms, to others' shame and grief, because they sometimes grievously wound their brothers with this sort of impudence. Now if we turn our eyes to the Lawgiver, who must in His own right rule our ears and heart no less than our tongue, we shall surely see that eagerness to hear detractions and unbecoming readiness to make unfavorable judgments are alike forbidden. For it is absurd to think that God hates the disease of evil speaking in the tongue, but does not disapprove of evil intent in the heart. Therefore, if there is any true fear and love of God in us, let us take care, as far as is possible and expedient and as love requires, not to yield our tongue or our ears to evil speaking and caustic wit and not to give our minds without cause to sly suspicion. But as fair interpreters of the words and deeds of all, let us sincerely keep their honor safe in our judgment, our ears, and our tongue.

12. The Golden Book of the Christian Life

From the Institutes of the Christian Religion, Book Three: The Way in Which We Receive the Grace of Christ. *Book Three includes Calvin's sensitive guide to the Christian life, a kind of little treatise of biblical counsel that is frank about the pain of life and yet offers a moving testimony to how the devout person can appreciate God's good gifts on earth, yet especially see through the veils of the present life and be sustained with joy in the hope of the resurrection. All of it is piety in daily practice.*

—E. A. McKee

The Life of the Christian

Now this scriptural instruction of which we speak has two main aspects. The first is that the love of righteousness, to which we are otherwise not at all inclined by nature, may be instilled and established in our hearts; the second, that a rule be set forth for us that does not let us wander about in our zeal for righteousness. . . .

And to wake us more effectively, Scripture shows that God the Father, as He has reconciled us to Himself in His Christ, has in Him stamped for us the likeness to which He would have us conform [Rom. 6:18]. . . .

For [the doctrine of the gospel] is a doctrine not of the tongue, but of life. It is not apprehended by the understanding and memory alone, as other disciplines are, but it is received only when it possesses the whole soul and finds a seat and resting place in the inmost affection of the heart.... We have given the first place to the doctrine in which our religion is contained, since our salvation begins with it. But it must enter our heart and pass into our daily living, and so transform us into itself that it may not be unfruitful for us....

I do not so strictly demand evangelical perfection that I would not acknowledge as a Christian one who has not yet attained it. For thus all would be excluded from the church, since no one is found who is not far removed from it, while many have advanced a little toward it whom it would nevertheless be unjust to cast away. What then? Let that target be set before our eyes at which we are earnestly to aim.... Let each one of us, then, proceed according to the measure of his puny capacity and set out upon the journey we have begun. No one shall set out so inauspiciously as not daily to make some headway, though it be slight. Therefore, let us not cease so to act that we may unceasingly make some progress in the way of the Lord. And let us not despair at the slightness of our success; for even though attainment may not correspond to desire, when today outstrips yesterday, the effort is not lost....

The Sum of the Christian Life: The Denial of Ourselves

Even though the law of the Lord provides the finest and best-disposed method of ordering a person's life, it seemed good to the heavenly Teacher to shape His people by an even more explicit plan to that rule which He had set forth in the law. Here, then, is the beginning of this plan: the duty of believers is "to present their bodies to God as a living sacrifice, holy and acceptable to Him" [Rom. 12:1], and in this consists the lawful worship of Him. From this is derived the basis of the exhortation that "they be not conformed to the fashion of this world, but be transformed by the renewal of their minds, so that they may prove what is the will of God" [Rom. 12:2]. Now the great thing is this: we are consecrated and dedicated to God in order that we may thereafter think, speak, meditate, and do nothing except to His glory. For a sacred thing may not be applied to profane uses without marked injury to Him....

We are not our own: let not our reason or our will, therefore, sway our plans and deeds. We are not our own: let us therefore not set it as our goal to seek what is expedient for us according to the flesh. We are not our own: insofar as we can, let us therefore forget ourselves and all that is ours.

Conversely, we are God's: let us therefore live for Him and die for Him. We are God's: let His wisdom and will therefore rule all our actions. We are God's: let all the parts of our life accordingly strive toward Him as our only lawful goal.

Oh, how much has that person profited who, having been taught that he is not his own, has taken away dominion and rule from his own reason that he may yield it to God! For, as consulting our self-interest is the pestilence that most effectively leads to our destruction, so the sole haven of salvation is to be wise in nothing and to will nothing through ourselves, but to follow the leading of the Lord alone. Let this therefore be the first step, that a person depart from himself in order that he may apply the whole force of his ability in the service of the Lord. I call "service" not only what lies in obedience to God's word, but what turns the mind of a person, empty of its own carnal sense, wholly to the bidding of God's Spirit.... But the Christian philosophy bids reason give way to, submit and subject itself to the Holy Spirit, so that the person may no longer live to himself, but have Christ living and reigning within him [Gal. 2:20].

From this also follows this second point: that we seek not the things that are ours, but those which are of the Lord's will and will serve to advance His glory. This is also evidence of great progress: that, almost forgetful of ourselves, surely subordinating our self-concern, we try faithfully to devote our zeal to God and His commandments. For when Scripture bids us leave off self-concern, it not only erases from our minds the yearning to possess, the desire for power and human favor, but it also uproots ambition and all craving for human glory and other more secret plagues. Accordingly, the Christian must surely be so disposed and minded that he feels within himself it is with God he has to deal throughout his life. In this way, as he will refer all he has to God's decision and judgment, so will he refer his whole intention of mind scrupulously to Him. For he who has learned to look to God in all things that he must do at the same time avoids all vain thoughts. This, then, is that denial of self which Christ enjoins with such great earnestness upon His disciples at the outset of their service....

For, after He proffered the grace of God to hearten us, in order to pave the way for us to worship God truly, He removed the two obstacles that chiefly hinder us: namely, ungodliness, to which by nature we are too much inclined, and second, worldly desires, which extend more widely.... Thus, with reference to both tables of the law, He commands us to put off our own nature and to deny whatever our reason and will dictate. Now He limits all actions of life to three parts: soberness, righteousness, and piety. Of these, soberness doubtless denotes chastity and temperance as well as a pure and frugal use of temporal goods and patience in poverty. Now righteousness embraces all the duties of equity in order that to each one may be rendered what is his own. There follows piety, which joins us in true holiness with God when we are separated from the iniquities of the world. When these things are joined together by an inseparable bond, they bring about complete perfection. But nothing is more difficult than, having bidden farewell to the reason of the flesh and having bridled our desires—nay, having put them away—to devote ourselves to God and our brethren and to meditate, amid earth's filth, upon the life of the angels....

Now, in these words we perceive that denial of self has regard partly to people, partly and chiefly to God. For when Scripture bids us act toward others so as to esteem them above ourselves and in good faith to apply ourselves wholly to doing them good, it gives us commandments of which our mind is quite incapable unless our mind be previously emptied of its natural feeling.... There is no other remedy than to tear out from our inward parts this most deadly pestilence of love of strife and love of self, even as it is plucked out by scriptural teaching. For thus we are instructed—to remember that those talents which God has bestowed upon us are not our own goods, but the free gifts of God, and any persons who become proud of them show their ungratefulness.... Let us, then, unremittingly examining our faults, call ourselves back to humility. Thus nothing will remain in us to puff us up; but there will be much occasion to be cast down. On the other hand, we are bidden so to esteem and regard whatever gifts of God we see in others that we may honor those people in whom they reside. For it would be great depravity on our part to deprive them of that honor which the Lord has bestowed upon them. But we are taught to overlook their faults, certainly not flatteringly to cherish them, but not on account of such faults to revile people whom we ought to cherish with goodwill and honor. Thus it will come about that, whatever person we deal with, we shall treat him not only moderately and modestly but also cordially and as a friend. You will never attain true gentleness except by one path: a heart imbued with lowliness and with reverence for others.

Now, in seeking to benefit one's neighbor, how difficult it is to do one's duty! Unless you give up all thought of self and, so to speak, get out of yourself, you will accomplish nothing here. For how can you perform those works that Paul teaches to be the works of love, unless you renounce yourself and give yourself wholly to others?...

But Scripture, to lead us by the hand to this, warns that whatever benefits we obtain from the Lord have been entrusted to us on this condition: that they be applied to the common good of the church. And therefore the lawful use of all benefits consists in a liberal and kindly sharing of them with others. No surer rule and no more valid exhortation to keep it could be devised than when we are taught that all the gifts we possess have been bestowed by God and entrusted to us on condition that they be distributed for our neighbors' benefit.... So too whatever a godly man can do he ought to be able to do for his brothers, providing for himself in no way other than to have his mind intent upon the common upbuilding of the church. Let this, therefore, be our rule for generosity and beneficence: we are the stewards of everything God has conferred on us by which we are able to help our neighbor, and we are required to render account of our stewardship. Moreover, the only right stewardship is that which is tested by the rule of love. Thus it will come about that we shall not only join zeal for another's benefit with care for our own advantage, but shall subordinate the latter to the former....

Scripture helps in the best way when it teaches that we are not to consider what people merit of themselves, but to look upon the image of God in everyone, [the image] to which we owe all honor and love. However, it is among members of the household of faith that this same image is more carefully to be noted, insofar as it has been renewed and restored through the Spirit of Christ. Therefore, whatever person you meet who needs your aid, you have no reason to refuse to help him. Say "he is a stranger"; but the Lord has given him a mark that ought to be familiar to you by virtue of the fact that He forbids you to despise your own flesh.

Say "he is contemptible and worthless"; but the Lord shows him to be one to whom He has deigned to give the beauty of His image. Say that you owe nothing for any service of his; but God, as it were, has put him in His own place in order that you may recognize toward him the many and great benefits with which God has bound you to Himself. Say that he does not deserve even your least effort for his sake; but the image of God, which recommends him to you, is worthy of your giving yourself and all your possessions. Now if he has not only deserved no good at your hand, but has also provoked you by unjust acts and curses, not even this is just reason why you should cease to embrace him in love and to perform the duties of love on his behalf. You will say, "He has deserved something far different of me." Yet what has the Lord deserved? Although He bids you forgive this person for all sins he has committed against you, He would truly have them charged against Himself.... We remember not to consider people's evil intention, but to look upon the image of God in them, which cancels and effaces their transgressions and with its beauty and dignity allures us to love and embrace them.

Now he who merely performs all the duties of love does not fulfill them, even though he overlooks none; but he, rather, fulfills them who does this from a sincere feeling of love.... Of Christians something even more is required than to show a cheerful countenance and to render their duties pleasing with friendly words. First, they must put themselves in the place of him whom they see in need of their assistance and pity his ill fortune as if they themselves experienced and bore it, so that they may be impelled by a feeling of mercy and humaneness to go to his aid just as to their own. The one who, thus disposed, proceeds to give help to his brethren will not corrupt his own duties by either arrogance or upbraiding. Furthermore, in giving benefits he will not despise his needy brother or enslave him as one indebted to himself. This would no more be reasonable than that we should either chide a sick member that the rest of the body labors to revive or consider it especially obligated to the remaining members because it has drawn more help to itself than it can repay. Now the sharing of tasks among members is believed to have nothing gratuitous about it, but rather to be a payment of that which, due by the law of nature, it would be monstrous to refuse.... Rather, each person will so consider with himself that in all his greatness he is a debtor to his neighbors, and that he ought in exercising kindness toward them to set no other limit than the end of his resources; these, as widely as they are extended, ought to have their limits set according to the rule of love.

Let us reiterate in fuller form the chief part of self-denial, which, as we have said, looks to God.... To begin with, then, in seeking either the convenience or the tranquility of the present life, Scripture calls us to resign ourselves and all our possessions to the Lord's will and to yield to Him the desires of our hearts to be tamed and subjugated.... First of all, let them neither desire, hope for, nor contemplate any other way of prospering than by the Lord's blessing. Upon this, then, let them safely and confidently throw themselves and rest....

To sum up, he who rests solely upon the blessing of God, as

it has been here expressed, will neither strive with evil arts after those things which people customarily madly seek after, which he realizes will not profit him, nor will he, if things go well, give credit to himself or even to his diligence, industry, or fortune. Rather, he will give God the credit as its Author. But if, while other people's affairs flourish, he makes but slight advancement or even slips back, he will still bear his low estate with greater equanimity and moderation of mind than some profane person would bear a moderate success which merely does not correspond with his wish. For he indeed possesses a solace in which he may repose more peacefully than in the highest degree of wealth or power. Since this leads to his salvation, he considers that his affairs are ordained by the Lord....

And for devout minds the peace and forbearance we have spoken of ought not to rest solely in this point, but it must also be extended to every occurrence to which the present life is subject. Therefore, he alone has duly denied himself who has so totally resigned himself to the Lord that he permits every part of his life to be governed by God's will. He who will be thus composed in mind, whatever happens, will not consider himself miserable or complain of his lot with ill will toward God. How necessary this disposition is will appear if you weigh the many chance happenings to which we are subject. Various diseases repeatedly trouble us: now plague rages; now we are cruelly beset by the calamities of war; now ice and hail, consuming the year's expectation, lead to barrenness, which reduces us to poverty; wife, parents, children, neighbors are snatched away by death; our house is burned

by fire. It is on account of these occurrences that people curse
their life, loathe the day of their birth, abominate heaven and the
light of day, rail against God, and, as they are eloquent in blasphemy, accuse Him of injustice and cruelty. But in these matters
the believer must also look to God's kindness and truly fatherly
indulgence.... The rule of piety is that God's hand alone is the
judge and governor of fortune, good or bad, and that it does not
rush about with heedless force, but with most orderly justice
deals out good as well as ill to us.

Bearing the Cross, a Part of Self-denial

But it behooves the devout mind to climb still higher, to the
height to which Christ calls His disciples: that each must bear his
own cross. For those whom the Lord has adopted and deemed
worthy of His fellowship ought to prepare for a hard, toilsome,
and unquiet life crammed with very many and various kinds
of evil. It is the heavenly Father's will thus to exercise them so
as to put His own children to a definite test. Beginning with
Christ, His firstborn, He follows this plan with all His children.
For even though that Son was beloved above the rest and in Him
the Father's mind was well pleased, yet we see that, far from being treated indulgently or softly, to speak the truth, while He
dwelt on earth, He was not only tried by a perpetual cross, but
His whole life was nothing but a sort of perpetual cross.... Why
should we exempt ourselves, therefore, from the condition to
which Christ our Head had to submit, especially since He sub-
mitted to it for our sake to show us an example of patience in

Himself? Therefore, the Apostle teaches that God has destined all His children to the end that they be conformed to Christ [Rom. 8:29]. Hence also in harsh and difficult conditions, regarded as adverse and evil, a great comfort comes to us: we share Christ's sufferings in order that as He has passed from a labyrinth of all evils into heavenly glory, we may in like manner be led through various tribulations to the same glory....

Besides this, our Lord had no need to undertake the bearing of the cross except to attest and prove His obedience to the Father. But as for us, there are many reasons why we must pass our lives under a continual cross.... He can best restrain this arrogance when He proves to us by experience not only the great incapacity but also the frailty under which we labor. Therefore, He afflicts us either with disgrace, poverty, bereavement, death, or other calamities. Utterly unequal to bearing these, insofar as they touch us, we soon succumb to them. Thus humbled, we learn to call upon His power, which alone makes us stand fast under the weight of afflictions.... Believers warned, I say, by such proofs of their diseases advance toward humility and so, sloughing off perverse confidence in the flesh, betake themselves to God's grace. Now when they have betaken themselves there, they experience the presence of a divine power in which they have protection enough and to spare.

That God has promised to be with believers in tribulation they experience to be true, while, supported by His hand, they patiently endure—an endurance quite unattainable by their own effort. The saints, therefore, through forbearance experience the fact that God, when there is need, provides the assistance that He has promised. Thence, also, is their hope strengthened, inasmuch as it would be the height of ingratitude not to expect that in time to come God's truthfulness will be as constant and firm as they have already experienced it to be....

The Lord also has another purpose for afflicting His people: to test their patience and to instruct them to obedience. Not that they can manifest any other obedience to Him save what He has given them. But it so pleases Him by unmistakable proofs to make manifest and clear the graces which He has conferred upon the saints, that these may not lie idle, hidden within. Therefore, by bringing into the open the power and constancy to forbear with which He has endowed His servants, He is said to test their patience.... But if God Himself does right in providing occasion to stir up those virtues which He has conferred upon His believers in order that they may not be hidden in obscurity—nay, lie useless and pass away—the afflictions of the saints, without which they would have no forbearance, are amply justified. They are also, I assert, instructed by the cross to obey, because thus they are taught to live not according to their own whim, but according to God's will....

Still, we do not see how necessary this obedience is to us unless we consider at the same time how great is the wanton impulse of our flesh to shake off God's yoke if we even for a moment treat that impulse softly and indulgently.... For not all of us suffer in equal degree from the same diseases or, on that account, need the same harsh cure. From this it is to be seen that some are tried by one kind of cross, others by another. But since the heavenly Physician treats some more gently but cleanses others by harsher remedies, while He wills to provide for the health of all, He yet leaves no one free and untouched, because He knows that all, to a person, are diseased.

Besides this, it is needful that our most merciful Father should not only anticipate our weakness, but also often correct past transgressions, so that He may keep us in lawful obedience to Himself.... Therefore, also in the very harshness of tribulations we must recognize the kindness and generosity of our Father toward us, since He does not even then cease to promote our salvation. For He afflicts us not to ruin or destroy us, but rather to free us from the condemnation of the world.... Scripture teaches that this is the difference between unbelievers and believers: the former, like slaves of inveterate and double-dyed wickedness, with chastisement become only worse and more obstinate. But the latter, like freeborn sons, attain repentance. Now you must choose in which group you would prefer to be numbered....

Now, to suffer persecution for righteousness' sake is a singular comfort. For it ought to occur to us how much honor God bestows upon us in thus furnishing us with the special badge of His soldiery. I say that not only they who labor for the defense of the gospel but they who in any way maintain the cause of righteousness suffer persecution for righteousness. Therefore, whether in declaring God's truth against Satan's falsehoods or in taking up the protection of the good and the innocent against the wrongs of the wicked, we must undergo the offenses and hatred of the world, which may imperil either our life, our fortunes, or our honor. Let us not grieve or be troubled in thus far devoting our efforts to God or count ourselves miserable in those matters in which He has with His own lips declared us blessed. Even poverty, if it be judged in itself, is misery; likewise exile, contempt, prison, disgrace; finally, death itself is the ultimate of all calamities. But when the favor of our God breathes upon us, every one of these things turns into happiness for us. We ought accordingly to be content with the testimony of Christ rather than with the false estimation of the flesh. So it will come about that we shall rejoice after the apostles' example, "whenever He will count us worthy to suffer dishonor for His name" [Acts 5:41].

What then? If, being innocent and of good conscience, we are stripped of our possessions by the wickedness of impious folk, we are indeed reduced to penury among people. But in God's presence in heaven our true riches are thus increased. If we are cast out of our own house, then we will be the more intimately received into God's family. If we are vexed and despised, we but take all the firmer root in Christ. If we are branded with disgrace and ignominy, we but have a fuller place in the kingdom of God. If we are slain, entrance into the blessed life will thus be open to us. Let us be ashamed to esteem less than the shadowy and fleeting allurements of the present life those things on which the Lord has set so great a value.

We are too ungrateful if we do not willingly and cheerfully undergo these things at the Lord's hand, especially since this sort of cross most properly belongs to believers.... Yet such a cheerfulness is not required of us as to remove all feeling of bitterness and pain. Otherwise, in the cross there would be no forbearance of the saints, unless they were tormented by pain and anguished by trouble. If there were no harshness in poverty, no torment in diseases, no sting in disgrace, no dread in death—what fortitude or moderation would there be in bearing them with indifference? But since each of these, with an inborn bitterness, by its very nature bites the hearts of us all, the fortitude of the believing person is brought to light if—tried by the feeling of such bitterness—however grievously he is troubled with it, yet valiantly resisting, he surmounts it....

You see that patiently to bear the cross is not to be utterly stupefied and to be deprived of all feeling of pain.... Yet we have nothing to do with this iron philosophy which our Lord and Master has condemned not only by His word, but also by His example. For He groaned and wept over both His own and others' misfortunes. And He taught His disciples in the same way: "The world," He said, "will rejoice; but you will be sorrowful and will weep" [John 16:20]. And that no one might turn it into a vice, He openly proclaimed, "Blessed are those who mourn" [Matt. 5:4]. No wonder! For if all weeping is condemned, what shall we judge concerning the Lord Himself, from whose body tears of blood trickled down [Luke 22:44]? If all fear is branded as unbelief, how shall we account for that dread with which, we read, He was heavily stricken? If all sadness displeases us, how will it please us that He confessed His soul "sorrowful even to death" [Matt. 26:38]?

I decided to say this in order to recall godly minds from despair, lest, because they cannot cast off the natural feeling of sorrow, they forthwith renounce the pursuit of patience. This must necessarily happen to those who make patience into insensibility and a valiant and constant person into a stock. For Scripture praises the saints for their forbearance when, so afflicted with harsh misfortune, they do not break or fall; so stabbed with bitterness, they are at the same time flooded with spiritual joy; so pressed by apprehension, they recover their breath, revived by God's consolation. In the meantime, their hearts still harbor a contradiction between their natural sense, which flees and dreads what it feels adverse to itself, and their disposition to piety, which even through these difficulties presses toward obedience to the divine will…. But the conclusion will always be: the Lord so willed; therefore let us follow His will. Indeed, amid the very pricks of pain, amid groaning and tears, this thought must intervene: to incline our heart to bear cheerfully those things which have so moved it.

Now, since we have taken the prime reason for bearing the cross from the contemplation of the divine will, we must define in a few words the difference between philosophic and Christian patience…. For if we obey God only because it is necessary, if we should be allowed to escape, we will cease to obey Him. But Scripture bids us contemplate in the will of God something far different: namely, first righteousness and equity, then concern for our own salvation….Therefore, in patiently suffering these tribulations, we do not yield to necessity, but we consent for our own good. These thoughts, I say, bring it to pass that, however much in bearing the cross our minds are constrained by the natural feeling of bitterness, they are as much diffused with spiritual joy. From this, thanksgiving also follows, which cannot exist without joy; but if the praise of the Lord and thanksgiving can come forth only from a cheerful and happy heart—and there is nothing that ought to interrupt this in us—it thus is clear how necessary it is that the bitterness of the cross be tempered with spiritual joy.

Meditation on the Future Life

Whatever kind of tribulation presses upon us, we must ever look to this end: to accustom ourselves to contempt for the present life and to be aroused thereby to meditate upon the future life....Then only do we rightly advance by the discipline of the cross, when we learn that this life, judged in itself, is troubled, turbulent, unhappy in countless ways, and in no respect clearly happy; that all those things which are judged to be its goods are uncertain, fleeting, vain, and vitiated by many intermingled evils. From this, at the same time, we conclude that in this life we are to seek and hope for nothing but struggle; when we think of our crown, we are to raise our eyes to heaven. For this we must believe: that the mind is never seriously aroused to desire and ponder the life to come unless it be previously imbued with contempt for the present life.

But let believers accustom themselves to a contempt of the present life that engenders no hatred of it or ingratitude against God. Indeed, this life, however crammed with infinite miseries it may be, is still rightly to be counted among those blessings of

God which are not to be spurned. Therefore, if we recognize in it no divine benefit, we are already guilty of grave ingratitude toward God Himself. For believers especially, this ought to be a testimony of divine benevolence, wholly destined, as it is, to promote their salvation. For before He shows us openly the inheritance of eternal glory, God wills by lesser proofs to show Himself to be our Father. These are the benefits that are daily conferred on us by Him. Since, therefore, this life serves us in understanding God's goodness, should we despise it as if it had no grain of good in itself? We must, then, become so disposed and minded that we count it among those gifts of divine generosity which are not at all to be rejected....

And this is a much greater reason if in it we reflect that we are in preparation, so to speak, for the glory of the heavenly kingdom. For the Lord has ordained that those who are one day to be crowned in heaven should first undergo struggles on earth in order that they may not triumph until they have overcome the difficulties of war and attained victory. Then there is another reason: we begin in the present life, through various benefits, to taste the sweetness of the divine generosity in order to whet our hope and desire to seek after the full revelation of this. When we are certain that the earthly life we live is a gift of God's kindness, as we are beholden to Him for it, we ought to remember it and be thankful. Then we shall come in good time to consider its most unhappy condition in order that we may indeed be freed from too much desire of it, to which, as has been said, we are of ourselves inclined by nature.

For if heaven is our homeland, what else is the earth but our place of exile? If departure from the world is entry into life, what else is the world but a sepulcher? And what else is it for us to remain in life but to be immersed in death? If to be freed from the body is to be released into perfect freedom, what else is the body but a prison? If to enjoy the presence of God is the summit of happiness, is not to be without this, misery? But until we leave the world "we are away from the Lord" [2 Cor. 5:6]. Therefore, if the earthly life is compared with the heavenly, it is doubtless to be at once despised and trampled underfoot. Of course it is never to be hated except insofar as it holds us subject to sin, although not even hatred of that condition may ever properly be turned against life itself. In any case, it is still fitting for us to be so affected either by weariness or hatred of it that, desiring its end, we may also be prepared to abide in it at the Lord's pleasure, so that our weariness may be far from all murmuring and impatience. For it is like a sentry post at which the Lord has posted us, which we must hold until He recalls us.... But in comparison with the immortality to come, let us despise this life and long to renounce it, on account of the bondage of sin, whenever it shall please the Lord.

But monstrous it is that many who boast themselves Christians are gripped by such a great fear of death, rather than a desire for it, that they tremble at the least mention of it, as of something utterly dire and disastrous. Surely, it is no wonder if the natural awareness in us bristles with dread at the mention of our dissolution. But it is wholly unbearable that there is not in Christian hearts any light of piety to overcome and suppress that fear, whatever it is, by a greater consolation.... If we should think that through death we are recalled from exile to dwell in the fatherland, in the heavenly fatherland, would we get no comfort from this fact?... Let us, however, consider this settled: that no one has made progress in the school of Christ who does not joyfully await the day of death and final resurrection.... Let us, then, take hold of a sounder view, and even though the blind and stupid desire of the flesh resists, let us not hesitate to await the Lord's coming, not only with longing, but also with groaning and sighs, as the happiest thing of all. He will come to us as Redeemer and, rescuing us from this boundless abyss of all evils and miseries, He will lead us into that blessed inheritance of His life and glory.

This is obvious: the entire company of believers, so long as they dwell on earth, must be "as sheep destined for the slaughter" to be conformed to Christ, their Head [Rom. 8:36]. They would therefore have been desperately unhappy unless, with mind intent upon heaven, they had surmounted whatever is in this world and passed beyond the present aspect of affairs.... For before their eyes will be that day when the Lord will receive His faithful people into the peace of His kingdom, "will wipe away every tear from their eyes," will clothe them with "a robe of glory ... and rejoicing" [Isa. 25:8; Rev. 7:17], will feed them with the unspeakable sweetness of His delights, will elevate them to His sublime fellowship—in fine, will deign to make them sharers in His happiness.... To conclude in a word: if believers' eyes are turned to the power of the resurrection, in their hearts the cross of Christ will at last triumph over the devil, flesh, sin, and the wicked.

How We Must Use the Present Life and Its Helps

By such elementary instruction, Scripture at the same time duly informs us what the right use of earthly benefits is—a matter not to be neglected in the ordering of our life. For if we are to live, we have also to use those helps necessary for living. And we also cannot avoid those things which seem to serve delight more than necessity. Therefore we must hold to a measure so as to use them with a clear conscience, whether for necessity or for delight. By His word the Lord lays down this measure when He teaches that the present life is for His people as a pilgrimage on which they are hastening toward the heavenly kingdom. If we must simply pass through this world, there is no doubt we ought to use its good things insofar as they help rather than hinder our course....

Let this be our principle: that the use of God's gifts is not wrongly directed when it is referred to that end to which the Author Himself created and destined them for us, since He created them for our good, not for our ruin. Accordingly, no one will hold to a straighter path than he who diligently looks to this end. Now if we ponder to what end God created food, we shall find that He meant not only to provide for necessity, but also for delight and good cheer. Thus the purpose of clothing, apart from necessity, was comeliness and decency. In grasses, trees, and fruits, apart from their various uses, there is beauty of appearance and pleasantness of odor. For if this were not true, the prophet would not have reckoned them among the benefits of God, "that wine gladdens a person's heart, that oil makes his face shine"

[Ps. 104:15]. Scripture would not have reminded us repeatedly, in commending His kindness, that He gave all such things to people. And the natural qualities themselves of things demonstrate sufficiently to what end and extent we may enjoy them. Has the Lord clothed the flowers with the great beauty that greets our eyes, the sweetness of smell that is wafted upon our nostrils, and yet will it be unlawful for our eyes to be affected by that beauty or our sense of smell by the sweetness of that odor? What? Did He not so distinguish colors as to make some more lovely than others? What? Did He not endow gold and silver, ivory and marble with a loveliness that renders them more precious than other metals or stones? Did He not, in short, render many things attractive to us apart from their necessary use?

Away, then, with that inhuman philosophy which, while conceding only a necessary use of creatures, not only malignantly deprives us of the lawful fruit of God's beneficence, but cannot be practiced unless it robs a person of all his senses and degrades him to a block. But no less diligently, on the other hand, we must resist the lust of the flesh, which, unless it is kept in order, overflows without measure.... First, one bridle is put upon it if it is determined that all things were created for us that we might recognize the Author and give thanks for His kindness toward us. Where is your thanksgiving if you so gorge yourself with banqueting or wine that you either become stupid or are rendered useless for the duties of piety and of your calling? Where is your recognition of God if your flesh boiling over with excessive abundance into vile lust infects the mind with its impurity so that you

cannot discern anything that is right and honorable? Where is our
gratefulness toward God for our clothing if in the sumptuousness
of our apparel we both admire ourselves and despise others, if
with its elegance and glitter we prepare ourselves for shameless
conduct? Where is our recognition of God if our minds are fixed
upon the splendor of our apparel? For many so enslave all their
senses to delights that the mind lies overwhelmed.... Therefore,
clearly, leave to abuse God's gift must be somewhat curbed, and
Paul's rule is confirmed: that we should "make no provision for
the flesh, to gratify its desires" [Rom. 13:14], for if we yield too
much to these, they boil up without measure or control.

Therefore, even though the freedom of believers in external
matters is not to be restricted to a fixed formula, yet it is surely
subject to this law: to indulge oneself as little as possible; but, on
the contrary, with unflagging effort of mind to insist upon cutting
off all show of superfluous wealth, not to mention licentiousness,
and diligently to guard against turning helps into hindrances.

The second rule will be: they who have narrow and slender
resources should know how to go without things patiently, lest
they be troubled by an immoderate desire for them. If they keep
this rule of moderation, they will make considerable progress in
the Lord's school.... To this end, then, let all those for whom the
pursuit of piety is not a pretense strive to learn, by the Apostle's
example, how to be filled and to hunger, to abound and to suffer
want [Phil. 4:12].

Besides, Scripture has a third rule with which to regulate the
use of earthly things. Of it we said something when we discussed

the precepts of love. It decrees that all those things were so given to us by the kindness of God and so destined for our benefit, that they are, as it were, entrusted to us, and we must one day render account of them. Thus, therefore, we must so arrange it that this saying may continually resound in our ears: "Render account of your stewardship" [Luke 16:2]. At the same time let us remember by whom such reckoning is required: namely, Him who has greatly commended abstinence, sobriety, frugality, and moderation and has also abominated excess, pride, ostentation, and vanity; who approves no other distribution of good things than one joined with love; who has already condemned with His own lips all delights that draw a person's spirit away from chastity and purity or befog his mind.

Finally, this point is to be noted: the Lord bids each one of us in all life's actions to look to his calling;... lest through our stupidity and rashness everything be turned topsy-turvy, He has appointed duties for every person in his particular way of life. And that no one may thoughtlessly transgress his limits, He has named these various kinds of living "callings." Therefore each individual has his own kind of living assigned to him by the Lord as a sort of sentry post, so that he may not heedlessly wander about throughout life....

It is enough if we know that the Lord's calling is in everything the beginning and foundation of well-doing. And if there is anyone who will not direct himself to it, he will never hold to the straight path in his duties. Perhaps, sometimes, he could contrive something laudable in appearance: but whatever it may be in the eyes of people, it will be rejected before God's throne. Besides, there will be no harmony among the several parts of his life. Accordingly, your life will then be best ordered when it is directed to this goal. For no one, impelled by his own rashness, will attempt more than his calling will permit, because he will know that it is not lawful to exceed its bounds. A person of obscure station will lead a private life ungrudgingly, so as not to leave the rank in which he has been placed by God. Again, it will be no slight relief from cares, labors, troubles, and other burdens for a person to know that God is his guide in all these things. The magistrate will discharge his functions more willingly; the head of the household will confine himself to his duty; each person will bear and swallow the discomforts, vexations, weariness, and anxieties in his way of life, when he has been persuaded that the burden was laid upon him by God. From this will arise also a singular consolation: that no task will be so sordid and base, provided you obey your calling in it, that it will not shine and be reckoned very precious in God's sight.

13. Correspondence with Prisoners

Calvin's understanding of pastoral care included the obliga-tion to seek to help those who were suffering for the faith. In 1552 five young men returning from their theological studies in Lausanne to be pastors in France were apprehended and imprisoned in Lyons. Over the following months Calvin and others corresponded with the prisoners and worked with people of goodwill, like the merchant John Liner, to try to free them. Although their faith was sustained, efforts to liberate the men failed, and in the spring of 1553 the five were burned at the stake. Soon several others who were also imprisoned, including Mathieu Dimonet and Denis Peloquin, followed their brothers to martyrdom.

—E. A. McKee

To the Five Prisoners of Lyons, Martial Eiba, Peter Escrivain, Charles Favre, Peter Naviheres, and Bernard Sequin: Geneva, 10 June 1552

My very dear Brethren, hitherto I have put off writing to you, fearing that if the letter fell into bad hands it might give fresh occasion to the enemy to afflict you. And besides I had been informed how God wrought so powerfully in you by His grace that you stood in no great need of my letters. However, we have not forgotten you, neither I nor all the brethren hereabouts, as to whatever we have been able to do for you. As soon as you were taken, we heard of it and knew how it had come to pass. We took care that help might be sent you with all speed and are now awaiting the result. Those who have influence with the prince in whose power God has put your lives are faithfully exerting themselves on your behalf, but we do not yet know how far they have succeeded in their suit. Meanwhile all the children of God pray for you as they are bound to do, not only on account of the mutual compassion which ought to exist between members of the same body, but because they know well that you labor for them in maintaining the cause of their salvation. We hope, come what may, that God of His goodness will give a happy issue to your captivity, so that we shall have reason to rejoice.

You see to what He has called you; doubt not therefore that according as He employs you He will give you strength to fulfill His work, for He has promised this and we know by experience that He has never failed those who allow themselves to be governed by Him. Even now you have proof of this in yourselves, for He has shown His power by giving you so much constancy in withstanding the first assaults. Be confident, therefore, that He will not leave the work of His hand imperfect. You know what Scripture sets before us to encourage us to fight for the cause of the Son of God; meditate upon what you have both heard and seen formerly on this head, so as to put it in practice. For all that I could say would be of little service to you, were it not drawn from this fountain. And truly we have need of a much more firm support than humans give to make us victorious over such strong enemies as the devil, death, and the world; but the firmness which is in Christ Jesus is sufficient for this, and all else that might shake us, were we not established in Him. Knowing, then, in whom ye have believed, manifest what authority He deserves to have over you.

As I hope to write to you again, I shall not at present lengthen my letter. I shall only reply briefly to the point which brother Bernard has asked me to solve. [Here the discussion of a number of theological issues is omitted.] ... I do not heap up quotations because these will be quite enough for your purpose. In conclusion, I beseech our good Lord that He would be pleased to make you feel in every way the worth of His protection of His own, to fill you with His Holy Spirit, who gives you prudence and virtue and brings you peace, joy, and contentment; and may the name of our Lord Jesus be glorified by you to the edification of His church!

To John Liner:
Geneva, 10 August 1552

Very dear Sir and Brother, we are all bound to give thanks to God for having made choice of you to assist our poor brethren who are detained in prison by the enemies of the faith and for having so strengthened you by the power of His Spirit that you spare no pains in so doing. I say that we are bound to give thanks to Him, for we must recognize this work as His, and that it is He alone who has disposed and directed you thereto. You have also reason to rejoice at the honor He has done you in employing you in so worthy and honorable a service and giving you grace to perform it. For however people despise and reject the poor believers who are persecuted for the sake of the gos-

pel, yet we know that God esteems them very pearls, that
there is nothing more agreeable to Him than our striving
to comfort and help them as much as in us lies. The Lord
Jesus declares that whatsoever shall have been done to one
of the least of His people will be acknowledged by Him
as done to Himself [Matt. 25:40]. How, then, if we have
furthered those who fight His battles? For such are, as it
were, His agents whom He appoints and ordains for the
defense of His gospel. Yea, He declares that a cup of water
given to them shall not be lost [Matt. 10:42]. If, then, you
have hitherto had the courage to present so goodly a sacrifice to God, strive to persevere. I know well that the devil
will not fail to whisper in your ear on many sides to divert
you from it, but let God prove the strongest, as it is fitting
He should. It is said that they who comfort the children
of God in their persecutions which they endure for the
gospel are fellow laborers for the truth [Philem. 1; 3; John
8]. Be content with this testimony, for it is no light matter
that God should uphold and approve us as His martyrs
even though we do not personally suffer, merely because
His martyrs are helped and comforted by us.

And therefore, although many tell you the contrary,
do not leave off so good a work or show yourself weary
halfway. I feel assured that you did not look to human
approval at the first; follow on then as the servant of Him
to whom we must cleave to the end. Reflect, moreover,
how many worthy brethren there are who glorify God
for what you are doing, who would be scandalized if
you altered your course. As for the dangers which they
set before you, I have no fear of their coming to pass, for

the good brethren for whom you have done so much feel themselves so indebted to you that, were they at liberty, far from being cowardly enough to betray you, they would expose themselves to death for your sake. You must also consider that by the support which they receive from you they are the more confirmed, for they have no doubt whatever that God has directed you to them, as indeed He has. And they have reason to lean still more firmly upon Him, seeing the paternal care He shows them. Be of good courage therefore in this holy work, in which you serve not only God and His martyrs but also the whole church.

Whereupon, my very dear sir and brother, after having heartily commended myself to you, I pray that our good Lord would increase you more and more with the gifts and riches of His Spirit, for the furtherance of His own honor; and meanwhile, that He would have you in His keeping.

John Calvin

To the Five Prisoners of Lyons:
Geneva, 15 May 1553

My very dear Brothers, we have at length heard why the herald of Bern did not return that way. It was because he had not such an answer as we much desired. For the king has peremptorily refused all the requests made by Messieurs of Bern, as you will see by the copies of the letters, so that nothing further is to be looked for from that quarter. Nay, wherever we look here below God has stopped the way. There is this good, however, that we cannot be frustrated of the hope which we have in Him and in His holy promises. You have always been settled on that sure foundation, even when it seemed as though you might have human help, and that we too thought so; but whatever prospect of escape you may have had by human means, yet your eyes have never been dazzled so as to divert your heart and trust, either on this side or that.

Now, at this present hour, necessity itself exhorts you more than ever to turn your whole mind heavenward. As yet, we know not what will be the outcome. But since it appears as though God would use your blood to sign His truth, there is nothing better than for you to prepare yourselves to that end, beseeching Him so to subdue you to His good pleasure that nothing may hinder you from following whithersoever He shall call. For you know, my brothers, that it behooves us to be thus mortified in order to be offered to Him in sacrifice. It cannot be but that you sustain hard conflicts in order that what was declared to Peter may be accomplished in you, namely, that they shall carry you whither you would not go [John 21:18]. You know, however, in what strength you have to fight—a strength on which all those who trust shall never be daunted, much less confounded. Even so, my brothers, be confident that you shall be strengthened according to your need by the Spirit of our Lord Jesus, so that you shall not faint under the load of temptations, however heavy it be—any more than He did, who won so glorious a victory that in the midst of our miseries it is an unfailing pledge of our triumph.

Since it pleases Him to employ you to the death in
maintaining His quarrel, He will strengthen your hands in
the fight and will not suffer a single drop of your blood to
be spent in vain. And though the fruit may not all at once
appear, yet in time it shall spring up more abundantly than
we can express. But as He has granted you this privilege,
that your bonds have been renowned and that the noise
of them has been everywhere spread abroad, it must be
(in despite of Satan) that your death should resound far
more powerfully, so that the name of our good God be
magnified thereby. For my part I have no doubt, if it please
this kind Father to take you unto Himself, that He has
preserved you hitherto in order that your long-continued
imprisonment might serve as a preparation for the better
awakening of those whom He has determined to edify by
your end. For let enemies do their utmost, they never shall
be able to bury out of sight that light which God has made
to shine in you in order to be contemplated from afar.

I shall not console or exhort you more at length, knowing that our heavenly Father makes you experience how
precious His consolations are and that you are sufficiently
careful to meditate upon what He sets before you in His
word. He has already so shown how His Spirit dwells
in you that we are well assured that He will perfect you
to the end. In leaving this world we do not go away at a
venture [haphazardly], as you know not only from the
certainty you have that there is a heavenly life, but also
because from being assured of the gratuitous adoption of
our God you go thither as to your inheritance. That God
should have appointed you as His Son's martyrs is a token

to you of superabounding grace. There now remains the conflict to which the Spirit of God not only exhorts us to go, but even to run. It is indeed a hard and grievous trial to see the pride of the enemies of truth so enormous, without its getting any check from on high; their rage so unbridled, without God's interfering for the relief of His people. But if we remember that, when it is said that our life is hid [Col. 3:3] and that we must resemble the dead, this is not a doctrine for any particular time but for all times, we shall not think it strange that afflictions should continue. While it pleases God to give His enemies the rein, our duty is to be quiet, although the time of our redemption tarries. Moreover, if He has promised to be the judge of those who have brought His people under thrall-dom, we need not doubt that He has a horrible punishment prepared, for such as have despised His majesty with such enormous pride and have cruelly persecuted those who call purely upon His name.

Put into practice then, my brethren, that precept of David's, that you have not forgotten the law of God [Ps. 119:61], although your life may be in your hands to be parted with at any hour. And seeing that He employs your life in so worthy a cause as is the witness of the gospel, doubt not that it must be precious to Him. The time draws nigh when the earth shall disclose the Blood which has been hid, and we, after having been disencumbered of these fading bodies, shall be completely restored. How-ever, let the name of the Son of God be glorified by our shame, and let us be content with this sure testimony, that we are persecuted and blamed only because we trust in the living God. In this we have wherewith to despise the whole world with its pride till we shall be gathered into that everlasting kingdom, where we shall fully enjoy those blessings which we now only possess in hope.

My brethren, after having humbly besought your re-membrance of me in your prayers, I pray our good God to have you in His holy protection, to strengthen you more and more by His power, to make you feel what care He takes of your salvation, to increase in you the gifts of His Spirit, to make them subserve His glory unto the end.

Your humble brother,
John Calvin

I do not make my special remembrances to each of our brethren because I believe that this letter will be common to them all. Hitherto I have deferred writing on account of the uncertainty of your state, fearing lest I might disquiet you to no purpose. I pray anew our good Lord to stretch out His arm for your confirmation.

ABOUT THE EDITOR

HarperCollins Spiritual Classics Series Editor Emilie Griffin has long been interested in the classics of the devotional life. She has written a number of books on spiritual formation and transformation, including *Clinging: The Experience of Prayer* and *Wilderness Time: A Guide to Spiritual Retreat*. With Richard J. Foster she coedited *Spiritual Classics: Selected Readings on the Twelve Spiritual Disciplines*. Her latest book is *Wonderful and Dark Is this Road: Discovering the Mystic Path*. She is a board member of Renovaré and leads retreats and workshops throughout the United States. She and her husband, William, live in Alexandria, Louisiana.

ABOUT MARILYNNE ROBINSON

Marilynne Robinson is the author of the novel *Housekeeping*, winner of the PEN/Hemingway Award, and *Gilead*, winner of the 2005 Pulitzer Prize, and the nonfiction works *The Death of Adam* and *Mother Country*. She teaches at the University of Iowa Writers' Workshop.

THE CLASSICS OF **WESTERN SPIRITUALITY**
A LIBRARY OF THE GREAT SPIRITUAL MASTERS

These volumes contain original writings of universally acknowledged teachers within the Catholic, Protestant, Eastern Orthodox, Jewish, Islamic, and American Indian traditions.

The Classics of Western Spirituality unquestionably provide the most in-depth, comprehensive, and accessible panorama of Western mysticism ever attempted. From the outset, the Classics has insisted on the highest standards for these volumes, including new translations from the original languages, and helpful introductions and other aids by internationally recognized scholars and religious thinkers, designed to help the modern reader to come to a better appreciation of these works that have nourished the three monotheistic faiths for centuries.

For more information on the
CLASSICS OF WESTERN SPIRITUALITY, **contact Paulist Press**
(800) 218-1903 • www.paulistpress.com